Letts
Study Aids

Physics 1

*Foundation Skills
for 11-14 year olds*

Barry Stone BSc

Head of Physics,
Vyne School,
Basingstoke

Charles Letts & Co Ltd.
London, Edinburgh & New York

First published 1986
by Charles Letts & Co Ltd
Diary House, Borough Road, London SE1 1DW

Design: Ben Sands
Illustrations: Roger Gorringe, Alex Murphy, Edward Ripley
Mumbles © Barry Stone 1986

ISBN 0 85097 656 1

Printed in Great Britain by
Charles Letts (Scotland) Ltd

Acknowledgements

The author and publishers are grateful to the following
individuals and organizations for permission to reproduce
photographs on which they hold the copyright:
Barnaby's Picture Library Figs. 7.1(d), 7.2, 7.4(a), 7.4(d), 10.4(a),
10.4(b); Barr and Stroud Ltd Figs. 21.1(a), 21.1(b); Anne Bolt
Figs. 7.3, 10.1, 21.2; British Airways Fig. 20.6; Jim Brownbill
Figs. 7.1(a), 7.1(b), 9.1(b), 10.4(c), 10.4(d), 11.2(a), 11.2(b), 11.2(c),
12.2(a), 12.2(b); Camera Press Ltd Figs. 5.1(b), 5.1(c), 5.1(d),
22.5(a); Central Press Photos Fig. 5.1(a); Comark Fig. 15.2(a);
Daily Telegraph Colour Library Fig. 13.2; John Hind Fig. 17.3;
Mansell Collection Figs. 5.2, 11.5; Jenny Matthews/Format Fig.
22.3; Milton Keynes Development Corporation Fig. 23.3;
Pilkington Fig. 15.2(b); David Reed/Sunday Times Magazine Fig.
22.7; Ann Ronan Picture Library Fig. 30.1; Salvation Army Fig.
22.6; Science Photo Library Figs. 7.4(b), 7.4(c), 9.1(a), 13.4, 20.2;
Shell International Petroleum Fig. 7.1(c); Space Frontiers Ltd Fig.
22.3; Elizabeth Whiting Fig. 21.3

Preface

Why Physics?

The first (and last) meeting with Physics is usually at school. School science, for good or bad, often blossoms under three main headings (even when hidden by the title – Combined Science): Chemistry, Biology and the 'other one'.

The first two sciences are easy to recognize. Chemicals are used every day in a typical household. Chemicals help with the washing up, make paints 'non-drip' and generally make themselves very useful. They are all around and usually quite easy to recognize. Biology is everywhere! Whether living or dead, plants, animals and microbes are all aspects of biology. One of nature's marvels is survival. Living things exist in the strangest places.

Physics doesn't have the same kind of instant image as Chemistry or Biology. Physics suffers because there is no easy way to describe what it is.

The purpose of this book is to emphasize and encourage an interest in, and to develop skills in, a science that is all around too – Physics. It is to support and reinforce science done at school in the three years (usually ages 11–14) before examination courses.

I am very grateful to David Bailey for his assistance with the preparation of this book. In addition I would like to thank Josephine Fageant for reading through the various Units, Tessa and Katie Crichton-Miller for trying out experiments and activities, Pat Rowlinson and her colleagues at Charles Letts & Co, Micro-style of Newbury for their help with computer facilities and lastly, 'Mumbles' for popping up all over the place.

Barry Stone 1986

4

Contents

Introduction

and guide to using the book

As children go through school they acquire a wide selection of skills. They spend many hours every day working and playing alongside others. This time is a preparation period for their future. Academic success in a particular area of study may be one of the goals to aim for.

Developments in science and technology are happening so fast it is impossible to keep up with them. Within a child's education there should be modern technology *and* basic science. They belong together. One of the more difficult tasks is to find a balance for them within the limitations of time and curriculum provided by any particular school. It is all too easy for the foundation skills of science to be skimmed over or missed out altogether.

Time is all too easily lost during the early years at school. Moving house, holidays during term time, changing schools, illness all reduce the time available to study a subject. Additionally, it may be that a particular child will benefit from more support in one or more areas of study.

Physics is a subject that can be fun, fascinating and occasionally frustrating. It is an area of study requiring skills and the understanding of certain concepts. As confidence grows, it becomes easier to make an objective decision whether or not to continue with it. Physics as an examination subject is a much sought after qualification. Entry to an examination course should only be made after much careful thought, and an important factor in this decision is a feeling of confidence in the subject.

This book is an aid for use at home. The Units introduce some skills and concepts and reinforce others. The book supplements, supports and enhances the work presented in Physics 'lessons'. As the book concentrates on Activities, it is ideal for filling in topics that have been missed, or for gaining expertise in handling simple equipment.

The aim in doing this is to provide a foundation for further study.

This volume is an integral part of the set of three. Particular care has been taken to include, in the three volumes, all the essential Physics required by pre-examination courses. Different schools will have different schemes of work. A school's timing of any particular piece of work may well not coincide with the order of contents in this series. Volumes 1 and 2 contain work that is more often found in secondary schools during the first two years. Volume 3 concentrates on work for the third year, during which examination courses are chosen. In some schools the third year is used to start such courses.

Foundation Skills in Physics is unlike many conventional text books in that it is based on skills and concepts, by way of Activities, designed to lead you through a topic from start to finish.

It is possible to use the book in several different ways:

(a) to support a school Physics course;
(b) to catch up work that has been missed;
(c) to pick out skills in need of practice and re-inforcement;
(d) for enjoyment.

Working through the book can be by Topic or Skill(s), chosen from the analysis table (page 8). Skills usually appear against more than one topic. Most of the Activity pages contain a considerable amount of practical work. They have been tried and can all be done at home. Certain experiments need to be done with care. These are indicated within the text.

Many topics contain a selection of Brainteasers. They are just that and will need some thought, though the solutions are usually straightforward.

Answers are not provided for all the questions in the Activities. Where they are not, solutions will be indicated in the text unless use of a library has been suggested (as one of the skills).

One of the skills of a practical subject is the ability to carry out experiments safely. Different hazards exist in different environments, and a child may need supervision with some of the Activities. Where it has been thought appropriate, safety warnings have been given in the text.

The skills listed in the analysis table (page 8) are based on the framework for Physics set by the Assessment of Performance Unit at the Department of Education and Science.

SKILLS

Unit		Reading & extracting information from				Expressing information & observations as				Use of instruments to measure/construct	Estimation skills	Observing accurately	Explaining what is observed	Ability to use/recognize patterns in information or readings	Ability to apply knowledge to a new situation	With reference to own or others investigation be able to				Use of, & introduction to, symbols terminology	Mathematical application
		Graphs	Tables	Charts/diagrams	Written passages	Graphs	Tables	Charts/diagrams	Written passages							Design	Critically assess	Perform	Describe		
1	Estimations		●	●							●									●	●
2	Mass			●				●	●	●										●	
3	Length & time		●		●		●		●	●	●			●				●	●	●	●
4	Volumes			●	●		●		●		●				●	●	●		●	●	●
5	Energy types			●					●											●	
6	Energy chains			●				●						●	●						
7	Food & fuels	●		●					●		●					●		●	●	●	●
8	Solid, liquids & gases			●				●		●		●	●		●			●	●		●
9	Surface tension & capillary action			●				●							●	●	●	●	●	●	
10	Naming forces			●								●	●		●			●	●		
11	Measuring forces			●						●	●				●					●	
12	Passing on forces			●				●							●	●		●	●		
13	Pairs of forces		●	●											●					●	
14	Measuring temperature	●		●		●	●				●				●					●	●
15	Thermometers			●		●	●		●						●			●	●		
16	Heating & cooling			●	●	●	●		●	●		●	●		●					●	●
17	Conduction – part 1		●	●	●	●	●		●		●				●	●		●		●	
18	Conduction – part 2			●	●				●			●	●		●	●	●	●	●		
19	Convection currents – part 1			●	●				●			●	●		●			●	●		
20	Convection currents – part 2			●	●				●						●	●		●			
21	Radiation			●					●			●			●	●	●	●	●		●
22	Insulators			●	●											●	●				
23	Heating houses		●	●	●		●									●					
24	Cells			●	●			●	●									●		●	
25	Circuit board project			●	●								●					●		●	
26	Circuits & switches			●	●						●						●	●			
27	Getting in the way			●	●										●			●		●	
28	Resistance & series circuits			●	●		●				●			●				●			
29	Resistance & parallel circuits			●	●		●				●			●				●			
30	Simple magnets				●										●			●		●	

CONCEPTS

Value of estimation in everyday life

Length, units
Mass, measuring devices; units
Time, time intervals; units
Volume, space occupied; units

Energy allows things to happen	Stored energy
Energy types; units	Energy cannot be created or
Energy changes	destroyed
Energy as molecular movement	Need for conservation

Molecules	Differences between solids,
Molecular structure	liquids, gases
The three states of matter	Forces of cohesion, adhesion
	Surface tension, capillary action

Forces as pushes, pulls, turns; units	Forces in pairs, action/reaction
Force transmission	Unbalanced forces causing
Weight as force due to gravity pulling down	changes, resultants

Temperature as hotness/coldness; units	Thermometers as measuring devices
Temperature scales	Physical change as reaction to
	temperature change, reversibility

Energy need for change of state, latent heat, specific heat; units
Relationship of energy need to: material, mass, temperature change
Heat transfer by conduction, convection as molecular movement
Heat transfer by radiation (as energy waves), passage through a
  vacuum
Infrared rays
Insulation

The cell as an energy source
Electricity flow, current
Complete circuits, series, parallel
Resistors, resistance; units

North, south poles, attraction, repulsion	Magnetic/non-magnetic materials
	Care of magnets

Unit 1

Estimations

1.1 Guessing games – the need for estimating

When do you leave home to get to school on time? How many miles further can you go before the car will need some more petrol or diesel fuel? How many rolls of wallpaper will you need to paper your bedroom?

Before you set out on a journey you make an estimation, a guess of how long it will take you to make sure that you arrive on time. You will probably play the same sort of guessing game with the number of rolls of wallpaper so that you buy just enough.

Much of Physics deals with taking measurements. These are usually done with simple tools that are easy to handle and read (for example, rulers, thermometers, clocks and watches). Guessing games, making estimations, are very important, even if you are very careful about taking measurements. Estimations give you an idea of size or amount, so you know what to expect. It would not be very clever to start cutting cloth for a dress pattern if you had no idea how much cloth was needed, or how much cloth you had!

1.2 Using our senses

When making guesses we try to use clues to help us. A man standing against a lorry gives us a clue to the size of the lorry because we know how big a man is. It is easy to be fooled! The diagrams in Fig. 1.1 are made to trick you into seeing something that is not there!

1.3 Units

Each measurement has its own special unit(s), such as:

Measurement	Units
Length	Kilometres (km)
	Metres (m)
	Centimetres (cm)
Temperature	Degrees Celsius (°C)
Time	Seconds (s)

Each time you make a guess it is very important to use the right units. If you wanted to know the length of a football pitch, an answer in

Fig. 1.1

centimetres or kilometres would not make much sense.

1.4 Some estimations

Length/distances/heights	Guess
Two storey house	9 m high
Football pitch	100 m long
Pencil	20 cm long
London–Newbury	110 km apart
A front door	2 m high
A milk bottle	20 cm tall

Time	Guess
To read this page	2 min (120 s)
To speak your name	2 s
To boil a kettle	4 min (240 s)
To load a games program	30 s

Temperature	Guess
A hot drink	60°C

Temperature and time are more difficult to estimate. What may feel cold to you may feel warm to someone else. Something that is interesting to you takes only a short time. Time seems to fly by. Something that you find uninteresting or boring can take forever.

Activities

Fig. 1.2

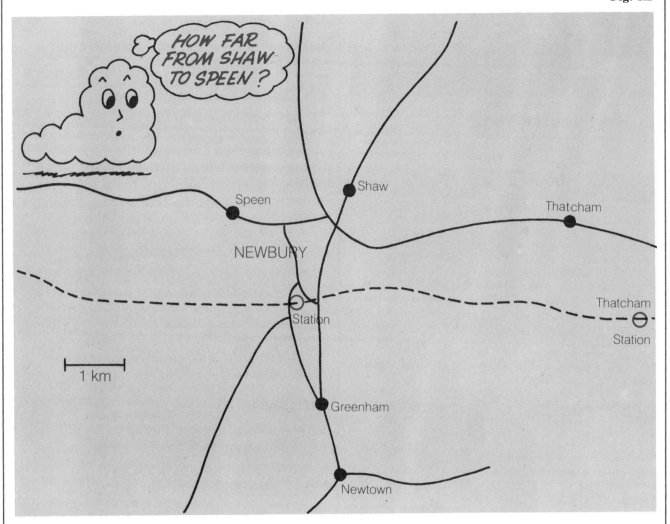

Newbury	07 37	07 55	08 32	09 00	10 18	10 35
Thatcham	07 44	08 00	08 39	09 05	......	10 40
Midgham	07 48	08 05	......	09 10	......	10 45
Aldermaston	07 52	08 09	......	09 14	......	10 49
Theale	07 58	08 15	......	09 20	......	10 55
Reading West	08 05	08 22	......	09 27	......	11 02
Reading	08 09	08 26	08 52	09 31	10 35	11 06
London Paddington	08 45	09 08	09 27	10 10	11 04	11 41

Fig. 1.3

The map in Fig. 1.2 shows part of the area around Newbury in Berkshire. Fig. 1.3 is a railway timetable for trains between Newbury and Paddington, London.

1 Using the map and a ruler to help you, estimate the following distances (to the nearest ½ kilometre):

(a) Newtown–Greenham
(b) Speen–Thatcham
(c) Newbury Station–Shaw

2 If you lived at Shaw how long would it take you to walk to a friend's house in Speen? (*Hint*: think how long it would take you to walk 1 km. A gentle walking pace is about 5 km per hour, or 1 km in 12 min.)

3 You want to catch the 07.55 train from Newbury to London, but you have to walk from Greenham. At about what time should you start your journey if you want to arrive at the station with 5 min to spare?

4 The Science Museum in London has a special video exhibition that opens to the public at 10.00 am. The journey to the museum from Paddington station takes about half an hour. Which would be the best train to catch from Newbury to be in time for the opening of the museum?

Summary

Estimates are guesses about measurements. They give us clues about what our accurate measurements should be.

Unit 2

Mass

2.1 How much is it worth?

Fig. 2.1

Mumbles the chef, in Fig. 2.1, has a problem with a recipe. As the kitchen scales have been mislaid there is no way to measure the ingredients so the amount of each item is not known.

An amount of material or 'stuff' is known as **mass**! It is measured in **kilograms** (kg).

A large object like a whale has a large mass and a small object like a coin has a small mass. Whatever mass you measure it has the same value all over the world, even in space too!

Often items in shops are sold in kilograms because it is easy to say exactly how much is wanted (for example, 1 kilogram of flour, 5 kilograms of potatoes).

2.2 Smaller parts of a kilogram

It is sometimes useful to use masses that are smaller than 1 kilogram. **kilo-** means thousand and so:

1 kilogram = 1 thousand grams
1 kg = 1000 g

Balances that are found in the home are usually marked in both grams (g) and kilograms (kg).

2.3 Large masses

Some things (such as lorries, large lumps of steel and heaps of sand) have their masses measured in tonnes:

1 tonne = 1000 kilograms

It is easier to talk about a 20 tonne lorry than a 20 000 kilogram lorry.

2.4 Using a balance

Fig. 2.2 shows the side of a lever-arm balance. These balances are easy to use, and you will probably have them at school. They sometimes have two scales, and to use them properly you have to choose the right scale. To use the smaller scale the counter-mass must be in PLACE A and to use the larger scale it must be in PLACE B.

2.5 The balance zero-screw

The scale should always read ZERO to start with. There is a special zero-screw at the bottom of the balance. This should be used to make sure the scale pointer shows 0 on the scale you are going to use *BEFORE* you start to take any measurements. If this is not done, any masses you measure will not be correct.

2.6 Scales

Until you are happy about using scales, take extra care to count the divisions carefully.

Fig. 2.2 Lever-arm balance

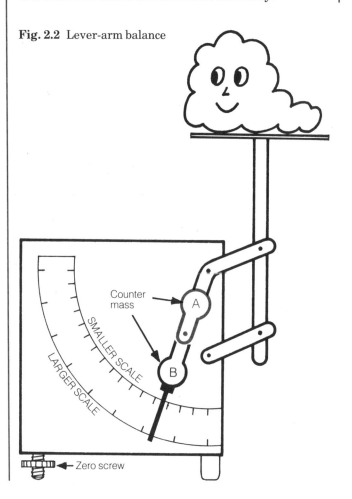

Activities

1 Guess the masses of these items from this list: 25 g, 500 g, 6 kg, 1 kg, 50 kg

(a) A bag of cement
(b) A baby
(c) A pot of jam
(d) A loaf of bread
(e) An airmail letter

2 We use kilograms more and more now as part of the metric system. There are still some of the old measurements in use. They are called 'imperial'. The imperial measures of mass are stones/pounds/ounces. Can you find out how many:

? ounces = 1 pound (lb)
? pounds = 1 stone

3 When you next go shopping look for some packets that are labelled in both 'kg' and 'lb'. Collect some of the wrappers and see if you can find a link between the pairs of numbers.

4 What are you worth in kg? What is your mass? Use some bathroom scales to measure your mass. Try it every morning for a week as soon as you get up. Be as accurate as you can. If you keep a record of your measurements you could make up a graph that will show how (if) your mass changes during the week.

5 There are many types of balance. How many of those in Fig. 2.3 can you name?

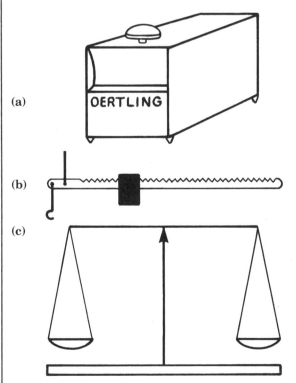

Fig. 2.3 What are they?

6 The four diagrams in Fig. 2.4 show parts of the scales of a lever-arm balance (see Fig. 2.2). In each diagram decide which scale should be used, and find the mass of each object.

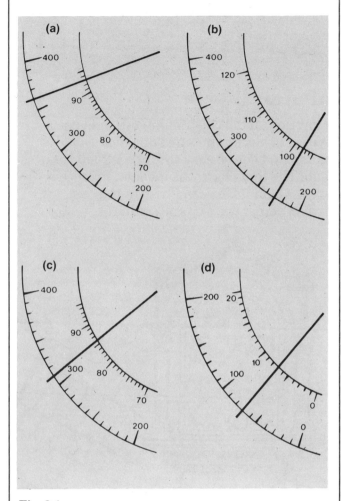

Fig. 2.4

7 If you have some kitchen scales at home try measuring the mass of some everyday objects and record them in a neat table.

Brainteaser

8 You have been given a bag with 100 marbles in it. One marble does not have enough mass to move the balance pointer. How do you find the mass of one marble?

Summary

The mass of an object is the amount of matter or 'stuff' in it. The mass of an object is always the same no matter where it is.

MASS is measured in kilograms (kg):
1 kg = 1000 g
1000 kg = 1 tonne

Unit 3

Length and time

3.1 Time

How do you tell the time? You would use a watch or clock! The same question would not have been so easy to answer 2000 years ago. The first clock was the sun. Primitive man would have seen it rise in the east, travel across the sky and set in the west.

This is a natural time period and he would have used a 'day' as his unit of time. The day is a long time and it is very useful to divide it up into smaller units. (The Egyptians used sticks in the ground as shadow clocks.) The idea of dividing daylight (the day) into 12 equal parts is very old. The summer has longer 'days' than winter, so it would have had longer hours too! This system of short and long hours lasted in Europe until the middle ages. It existed in Japan until the nineteenth century. Dividing up the night is a more difficult task.

Usually time measurements in physics are made in seconds. Fig. 3.1 shows a number of ways of measuring time. How many can you name?

Fig. 3.1 What are these called?

3.2 Fast and slow

When you go to the cinema, the films appear to move and yet they are made up of many still pictures. The pictures are changing so quickly your eye cannot keep up with them. They change 24 times every second. Television pictures change 25 times every second.

Using cine film is one method of recording events that happen quickly. Once the film has been made it can be projected in slow motion, and the details of the event can be seen more clearly.

A stroboscope is a special kind of flashing light. When this is used with a camera many images can be recorded on one frame of film. This method of freezing movement is called stroboscopic photography.

3.3 Length

Throughout history there have been many different units of length. Elizabeth I used her own 'yard' of length, which was different from the 'yard' used by Henry VII. They are both different from the 'yard' that is still used sometimes today. Various parts of the body have been used as units of length, for example, forearm, foot. Horses are measured in hands!

The standard unit of length is the **metre** (m). There is enough room for 10 000 000 metre-rulers to be laid end-to-end between the North pole and the Equator!

$$1000 \text{ metres (m)} = 1 \text{ kilometre (km)}$$
$$1 \text{ m} = 100 \text{ centimetres (cm)}$$
$$1 \text{ cm} = 10 \text{ millimetres (mm)}$$

3.4 Using a ruler

There are right and wrong ways to use a simple ruler. These are shown in Fig. 3.2.

Fig. 3.2

Activities

1 Fill in the missing numbers. The first one has been completed for you.

(a) 200 cm = 2 m
(b) ... mm = 10 cm
(c) ... m = 1½ km
(d) ... mm = 74 cm
(e) ... cm = 1¼ m
(f) ... s = 2 min
(g) ... min = 3 hours
(h) ... s = ½ hour

2 Try this simple experiment. It is to test your reactions. The only equipment needed for this is a ruler and the help of a friend. Fig. 3.3 shows you how to arrange yourselves and the ruler. As one person drops the ruler the other tries to catch it with their fingers.

Measure the distance from the bottom of the ruler to where it has been caught. Some reaction times are shown in Table 3.1. If your measurements are between those shown, can you estimate any time differences?

Distance fallen	Time taken
5 cm	0.10 s
10 cm	0.14 s
15 cm	0.17 s
20 cm	0.20 s
25 cm	0.22 s

Table 3.1

3 Here are some devices used for measuring time:
Pulse
Wrist watch with a second hand
Stopwatch
Candle
Lap timer
Which would be the most suitable for measuring the following?

(a) Time to read Section 3.2
(b) A full-length video film
(c) Time to load from tape this page as a computer program
(d) The time of a 100 metre dash
Can you say why you chose each measuring device?

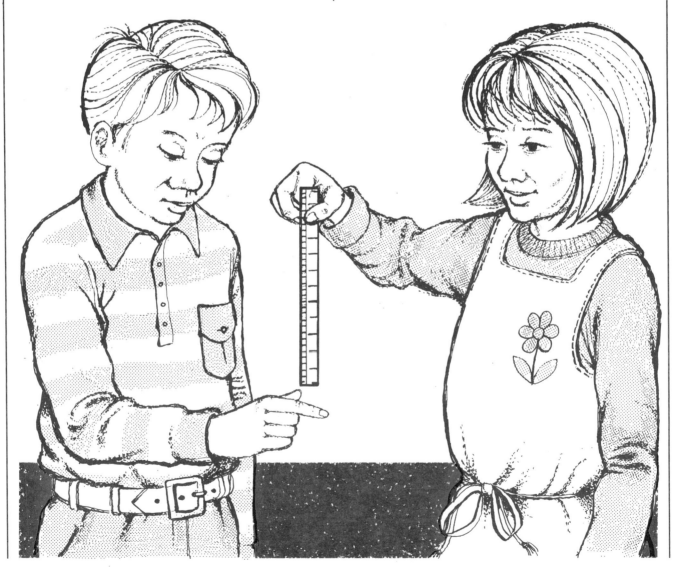

Fig. 3.3 Timing your reactions

4 Use a ruler to measure these items, but estimate them first. Draw out a table like the one below, and record your results in it.

Object	Guess	Measurement
My height		
A pencil		
A comic		
A film slide		

Brainteasers

5 This book has many pages in it. Can you find a way to measure the thickness of one page?

6 Make a pendulum clock. You will need:
   about 1.5 metres of string
   a small mass
   some kind of stop-watch
Make up a pendulum like the one in Fig. 3.4, and start it swinging gently. (One complete swing is all the way across and back again!)

Measure the length of the pendulum. Using the stop-watch, measure the time taken for 10 complete swings. Now work out the time taken for one complete swing (the period). Draw out a Table like this and record your results in it.

Length of pendulum (in m)	Time for 10 swings	Time for 1 swing (period)

Try the experiment again with a different length of string. Can you make it swing so that the period is 2 seconds? What do you notice about the length of the string? What can you make using a pendulum like this?

7 Why are grandfather clocks so tall?

Summary

Long and short time periods are easy to measure if the right type of timing device is used. There are right and wrong ways to use even simple instruments, such as rulers.

Fig. 3.4

Unit 4

Volumes

4.1 Space

Volume just means space! Any object you can think of takes up space. Everything has a volume. You have volume because you take up space. Even outer space has volume too! Volumes come in all shapes and sizes. There are neat shapes like boxes, and there are awkward shapes like milk bottles.

4.2 Volume

Volume is usually measured in **cubic metres** (m^3) or **cubic centimetres** (cm^3). Fluids (liquids and gases) are also measured in **litres** (l) and **millilitres** (ml).

$$1 \, m^3 = 1 \text{ million } cm^3$$
$$1 \text{ litre} = 1000 \text{ ml} = 1000 \, cm^3$$
$$1 \text{ ml} = 1 \, cm^3$$

In the building trade, sand is ordered by the 'cubic metre' not by the kilogram. 1 m^3 of wet sand has much more mass than 1 m^3 of dry sand, but it contains the same amount of sand!

4.3 Kitchen measures

At home liquids are usually measured in litres

1 litre (l) of water has a mass of 1 kg
1 millilitre of water has a mass of 1 g

4.4 Finding the volume of regular shapes

Boxes, cans and balls are examples of regular shapes. Their volumes can all be found quite quickly by measurement. The easiest is the box shape. Any large volume can be thought of as a lot of small volumes put together, like the example in Fig. 4.1.

The box in Fig. 4.1 is made up of:
Length – 4 cm (4 rows)
Width – 3 cm (3 rows)
Height – 2 cm (2 rows)
The volume (V) = Length × Width × Height
$$(V) = 4 \text{ cm} \times 3 \text{ cm} \times 2 \text{ cm}$$
$$V = 24 \, cm^3$$

Fig. 4.1 How many?

Fig. 4.2 What is the value here?

4.5 Finding the volumes of liquids

Using a measuring cylinder is the easiest way to do this. It is normally marked in cm^3 or ml. Fig. 4.2 shows you how to read the volume value.

At the top of a liquid a curved surface appears by the edge of the container. This curve is called the **meniscus**. This can fool you about the real level of the liquid!

4.6 Finding the volume of irregular shapes

Cups, toys and most kinds of sweets are examples of irregular shapes. It is very easy to find their volume. First a measuring cylinder needs to be filled with an 'easy to read' amount of water, perhaps 50 ml. The shape has to be added so that it is completely underwater. The DIFFERENCE in these two values is the same as the volume of the shape. Sugar will dissolve in water and so another liquid (such as methylated spirits) has to be found for this solid.

Activities

1 Find the volumes of the shapes shown in Fig. 4.3. Use this equation:

volume = length × width × height

(A calculator might help!)

2 Collect some regular everyday objects (box shapes) and measure their three sides to the nearest centimetre. It does not really matter which side you call length or width or height, as long as you measure the three different sides. Put the values into a table like the one below and find their volumes.

Object	Length (cm)	Width (cm)	Height (cm)	Volume (cm³)
Book				
Cassette box				
Pen case				
?				

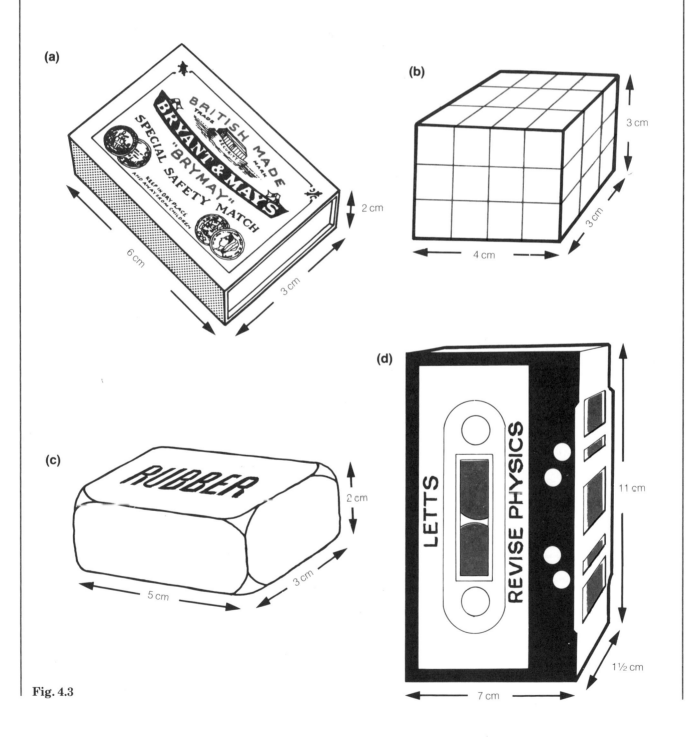

(a)

2 cm

6 cm

3 cm

(b)

3 cm

3 cm

4 cm

(c)

RUBBER

2 cm

5 cm

3 cm

(d)

LETTS REVISE PHYSICS

11 cm

1½ cm

7 cm

Fig. 4.3

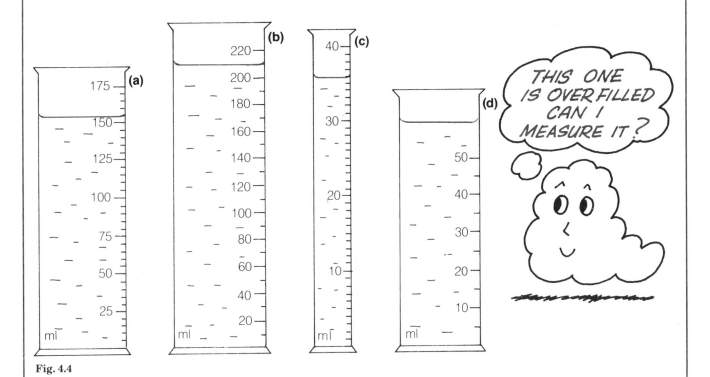

Fig. 4.4

3 When you are next in a supermarket look at the items that are sold by volume. Do any sizes appear more often than others? Are there any common sizes?

4 Can you think of any reasons why perfume and after-shave are sold in small bottles?

5 Many shops sell computer games. Some of the game boxes are very different in size from their cassette boxes. Why do you think this is?

6 What do Section 4.6 and 'you having a bath' have in common?

7 How would you find the volume of a small balloon or a piece of cork that floats?

8 There are other units that volume can be measured in. How many can you find?

9 What do firkins, barrels and hogsheads have in common?

10 Coins do not take up much space unless you have a pocketful. Can you think of a way to work out the volume of a single coin?

11 What are the volumes shown on the measuring cylinders in Fig. 4.4?

Brainteaser

12 Charles, another chef, has only two jugs. All he knows is that one jug holds 7 litres and the other 3 litres. He needs to measure out exactly 4 litres of water and then exactly 8 litres of water. He cannot do it. Can you help him with these two problems?

Summary

Everything takes up space.
Volumes are a measure of space or capacity.

Unit 5

Energy types

5.1 What is energy?

It is almost impossible to say what energy is! No one can really tell you! No one really knows! You cannot go out and collect some or go into a shop and buy pure energy. What is possible is to show you what energy does.

**Energy allows you to do things!
Energy can make things happen!**

If you can walk, run, talk, sing, ride a bike or even eat your breakfast, then you use energy. (You use energy to eat, but at the same time you are taking in more energy.) Almost everything has some energy (see Fig. 5.1).

5.2 Energy names

There are many names given to energy. You can think of them as different names for varieties of the same thing.

(a) Light energy: this is energy that can be seen. It travels in waves and is a member of a much larger family of energies that includes X-rays, infrared waves and radio waves. It is impossible to store because it radiates away.

(b) Heat energy: this label can be thought of in two ways.

(i) First a wave, called **infrared** (IR), which travels from place to place carrying energy from hot things to cooler things. It is difficult to store, because it 'leaks' away. The largest source of this heat energy nearby is the sun.

(ii) The second use of this label is for the shaking or movement of the molecules in a material. A red-hot poker has a lot of heat stored in it because its molecules are shaking violently. As it cools it gives away some of its heat energy as infrared waves. You can feel them if you put your hand nearby!

(c) Sound energy: this also travels in waves. (They are **very** different kinds of waves called **vibrations**.) They carry energy from louder places to quieter places.

(d) Electrical energy: this is energy carried by a flow of electricity. It is the most useful variety of energy.

(e) Magnetic energy: this can be found in magnetic materials.

(f) Kinetic energy: this is the energy of movement. Anything that moves has some kinetic energy.

(g) Potential energy: is any kind of energy that is stored. Electricity that is stored in a battery would be called 'potential-electrical energy', meaning stored electrical energy. Foods and fuels store energy in the form of chemicals and they would be called 'potential-chemical energies'.

Objects have stored energy if they are high up and able to fall because of gravity. They have potential energy. The energy that is stored in the water behind a dam wall is 'potential-gravitational energy' (because gravity would cause the water to fall if the dam wall were not there).

(h) Atomic or **nuclear energy:** this is stored by materials such as uranium. It is used in power stations.

5.3 Units of energy

Energy is measured in units called **joules** (J). If you consider that a lettuce leaf provides you with about 10 joules of energy then this gives you some idea of what one joule is worth!

Fig. 5.1 What energies are being used in these photos? (*continued on next page*)
Fig. 5.1 (a) (*Opposite*) An airship
Fig. 5.1 (b) (*Above*) A 'maglev' train which is raised above the rails by magnetic repulsion

Unit 5 continued

continued

Fig. 5.1 (c) A dragster capable of speeds up to 500 km per hour. The parachute acts as a brake.
Fig. 5.1 (d) A rock concert

Activities

1 PHYSICS IN HISTORY Read this and then answer the questions that follow.

James Prescott Joule

J P Joule was not a professional scientist. He was a Manchester brewer. When he was 19 he built an electric motor and measured the input and output of energy. He was trying to see if it would replace the steam engine. The idea was not very practical as he found that a kilogram of zinc (from the battery) allowed the motor to do the same work as only 200 grams of coal in the steam engine!

Joule then built a dynamo and discovered that the electric current produced heat when he turned the winding handle. He wondered if the heat could be measured, and so he covered the dynamo in water and measured its change in temperature.

From this experiment he wondered if it was possible to convert work (like the hard work done in turning the winding handle) straight into heat without first making electricity.

He worked for 40 years and during this time he built some of the finest equipment used to investigate the link between work and heat. Some of this equipment is at the Science Museum in London.

Joule was a very enthusiastic scientist and when he went on honeymoon to Switzerland he took a thermometer. Lord Kelvin found him measuring the temperature at the top and bottom of a tall waterfall (Fig. 5.2).

Fig. 5.2

(a) How old was James Joule when he made his first electric motor?

(b) Why did he build it?

(c) What did he discover about his motor?

(d) What two things was he trying to link together?

(e) What is the physical unit named after him, and what does it measure?

Brainteaser

(f) Would you expect the temperature at the top of a waterfall to be higher or lower than at the bottom – and why?

2 The cinema was once known as the KINEMA. Can you think of a reason why?

3 WORDSEARCH. Hidden in the block of letters are 10 words to do with energy. They could be found in any direction.

M	O	V	E	M	E	N	T	W	E	S	Y
W	K	S	F	H	Y	U	D	K	L	L	R
D	I	G	I	K	W	C	V	A	E	A	C
L	N	T	H	G	I	L	T	K	C	I	I
S	E	F	T	M	P	E	E	W	T	T	T
A	T	O	M	I	C	A	F	Q	R	N	E
C	I	G	S	T	O	R	E	D	I	E	N
J	C	H	E	M	I	C	A	L	C	T	G
K	E	G	A	Y	E	N	F	T	A	O	A
T	R	S	D	N	U	O	S	J	L	P	M

Summary

There are many varieties of energy. They all allow you 'to do something'.
James Joule found that it was not possible to create or destroy energy; you can only change it from one kind into another.

Unit 6

Energy chains

6.1 Energy chains

Energy exists all around us even though it may be difficult to spot sometimes. You cannot make any more energy and you cannot destroy what is already about. It will not let you do either! Energy would seem to be rather crafty. If you try to destroy it, or use it up, all it will do is change into some other kind. If you try to make some you will find that you have to use some to start with! The changing or one kind of energy into another is known as an **energy chain**. Fig. 6.1 shows some of the different kinds of energy linked together. Energy can flow very happily from one to another in any direction.

It is often easier to spot an energy chain than a single example of energy. A car driving along the road changes potential-chemical energy (petrol/diesel) into kinetic (moving) energy. A plane also uses potential-chemical energy as part of its energy chain, but it has to change some of this into potential energy as well because a plane has to fly in the air.

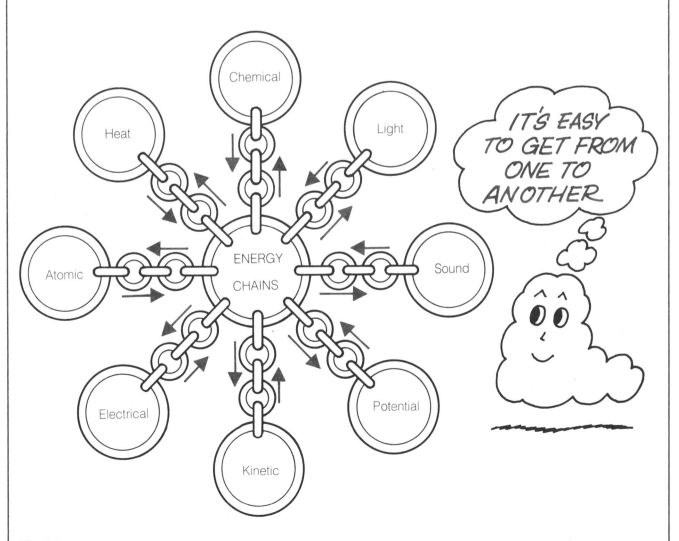

Fig. 6.1

Unit 6 continued

6.2 Energy arrows

Fig. 6.2 is an energy arrow. It shows how an energy chain works. The cyclist has some chemical energy to start with in his muscles. He changes this into kinetic energy as he rides along, but some is wasted and he and his muscles get hot.

6.3 Wasted energy

No matter what energy chain you use, some of the energy will be wasted. It will be turned into heat which is often no use at all. Sometimes it can even be a very great nuisance. If a car engine really overheats it could stop working altogether, seize up, and be ruined. If something does not waste very much energy then it is **efficient** at converting energy. The more energy that is wasted the less efficient a machine becomes.

Fig. 6.2 An energy arrow

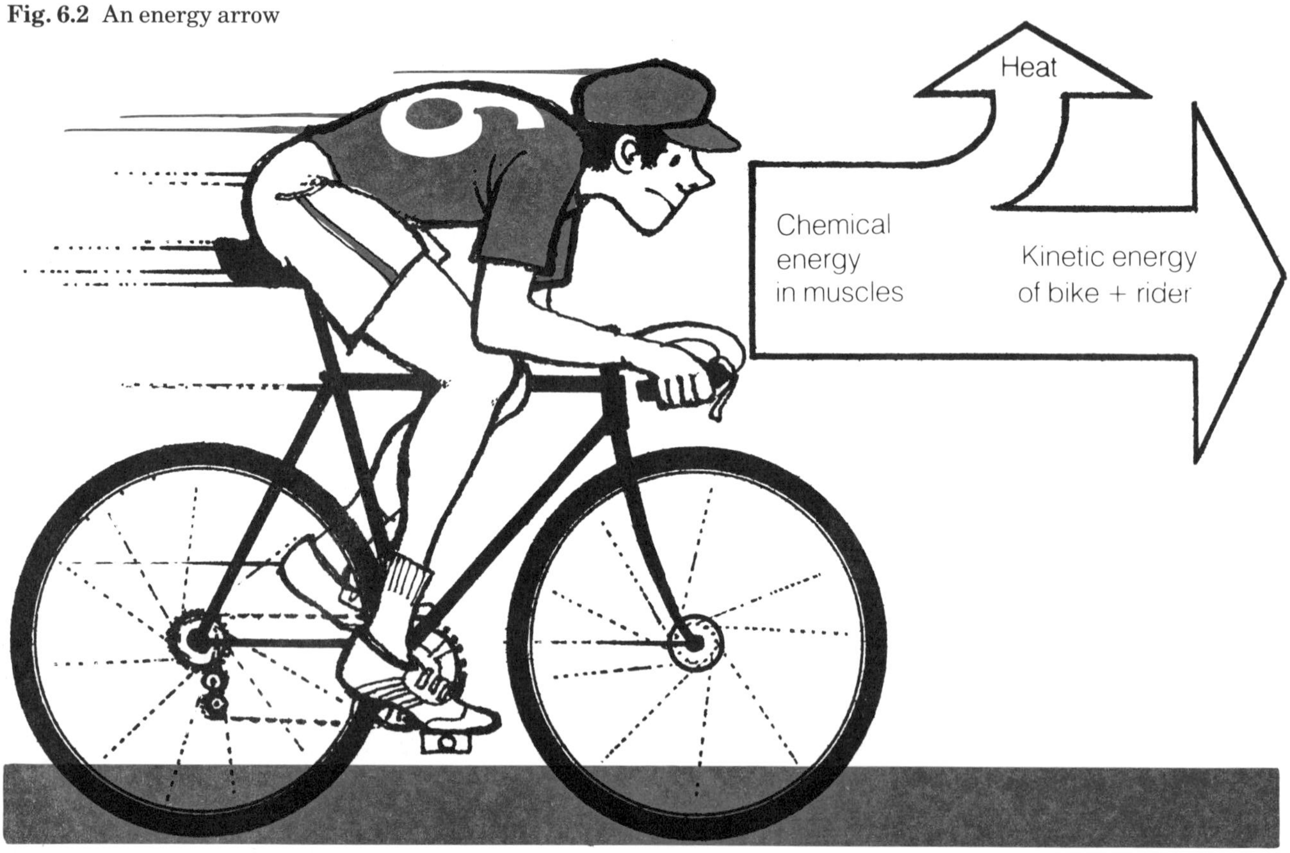

Heat

Chemical energy in muscles

Kinetic energy of bike + rider

Activities

1 In (a), (b) and (c) in Fig. 6.3 the diagrams have become mixed up. Can you rearrange the order of each set of four so that the diagrams follow one another in a sensible order?

2 Pair up these lists correctly:

Object	Main energy change
A battery	Electrical to potential
An electric motor	Electrical to light and sound
Lift	Chemical to kinetic
Solar cell	Chemical to heat and light
Radio	Atomic to electrical
TV	Electrical to light
Torch	Light to electrical
Car	Chemical to electrical
Fire	Electrical to kinetic
Nuclear power station	Electrical to sound

Fig. 6.3

3 Energy changers are all around the home. Can you name some machines that will change energy from:

(a) electrical to heat
(b) electrical to sound and kinetic
(c) electrical to heat and kinetic
(d) electrical to kinetic
(e) chemical to heat and light

4 Fig. 6.4 shows three energy arrows, but they have some of their labels missing. Redraw them and complete them.

5 Draw energy arrows to show the main energy changes that take place in:

(a) A portable radio
(b) A clockwork toy
(c) A tumble dryer
(d) An electric drill
(e) An electronic calculator
(f) A match

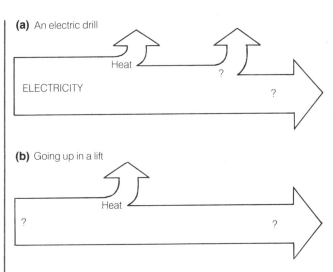

(a) An electric drill

(b) Going up in a lift

(c) A skydiver 'going down'

Fig. 6.4

Summary

Energy cannot be made or destroyed.
Energy can be changed from one kind to another very easily.
When an energy change happens some energy is always wasted as heat.

Unit 7

Foods and fuels

7.1 Fuels found naturally

All around us are fuels that will supply us with energy. We just have to look carefully for them (Fig. 7.1). Not all fuels are to be found in the ground, although many of the more abundant ones are.

7.2 Peat

The Scottish Highlands and Ireland are rich in peat, which is often used as a fuel. It can be made from heather or decayed vegetable matter. It is dark brown, looking something like soil. The peat is cut from the marshy ground and then stacked to dry. When it burns it does so very slowly. The smoke has a pleasant smell.

7.3 Coal

Millions of years ago, parts of the earth were covered with vast forests and areas of vegetation. These eventually became covered in mud, sand and rocks. This mass of material crushed the wood and vegetation and compressed it into thin layers. We now call these layers 'seams of coal' (Fig. 7.2).

The type of coal in a seam depends on how much

Fig. 7.1

Fig. 7.2 Modern underground coal mining

Fig. 7.3 Asphalt pool in Trinidad

it was crushed in the first place. One kind of soft brown coal is called lignite. It has a texture something like wood and is found in Australia and Germany. A much harder, darker kind of coal is known as anthracite. This type of coal is suitable for domestic fires and power stations.

7.4 Coal, coke and coal gas

If coal is heated carefully so that it does not burn, it gives off a gas. This is known as coal gas. (Coal gas was used as the main domestic gas fuel until recently. It was replaced by the natural gas from under the North Sea.) What remains of the coal is a hard, dark, porous substance called coke.

7.5 Oil

Another very important type of fuel is oil. This too was formed millions of years ago, but this was made from plants and animals which settled and decayed on the ocean floors. In the same way that coal was formed by crushing, so too was the oil. In some parts of the world the oil has started to seep onto the surface (Fig. 7.3) to form pools of thick natural asphalt.

Natural gas always appears on top of the deposits of oil. If this gas is under enough pressure, it will force the oil to the surface when a well is sunk into it. If the gas pressure is not strong enough, the oil must be pumped up.

7.6 Fractions

When oil emerges from the ground it looks nothing like the oils that we use every day. Crude oil is a mixture of many different chemicals. Some of these are very thick and some are very thin. They have to be separated. This separation is done at a refinery by a process known as **fractionation**. There the oil is split into different **fractions** by heating it to higher and higher temperatures.

Fraction	Boiling point	Uses
Calor gas	40°C	Portable cookers and stoves
Petrol	40–170°C	Cars
Paraffin	150–240°C	Jet engines
Diesel oil	220–240°C	Heavy trucks and lorries
Light oil	250–300°C	Oiling clocks, hinges
Heavy oil	300–350°C	Oiling heavy machinery
Tar and wax	above 350°C	Making roads

7.7 Foods

These are examples of fuels. All animals need to take in fuel regularly. When human beings take in too much, they become fat because the body is able to store the excess energy. Being 'overweight' is to be avoided. Going on a diet by 'counting the calories' is a common occurrence.

Energy, we know, is measured in joules, yet we talk of calorie-counting. They are from two systems of units and are very simply related:

1 calorie = 4.20 joules

Unit 7 continued

7.8 Energy values

Different foods provide different amounts of energy. The amount of energy provided by a kilogram of food is known as the energy value or 'calorific value'. Tables 7.1 and 7.2 list the approximate energy values for some common foods and fuels. These have been given in **kilojoules** per 100 g (100 g is an average-sized portion of food).

Fuel	Calorific value
Coal	3000
Peat	2500
Wood	1700
Anthracite	3500
Petrol	4300
Natural gas	5600

Table 7.2 Calorific value of some fuels (in kilojoules per 100 g)

Proteins		Carbohydrates		Fats		Other	
Cheese	1680	Chocolate	2300	Butter	3000	Potatoes	350
Lean meat	1200	Sugar	1600	Margarine	3000	Peas	400
Eggs	700	Brown bread	1000	Olive oil	3000	Fruit (fresh)	200
Liver	600			Fatty meat	3000	Green vegetables	150
Fish	300						

Table 7.1 Calorific value of some foods (in kilojoules per 100 g)

7.9 Future energy sources

Fuels from the North Sea will not last forever, and there is always a need to find other sources of energy. It is also important that energy is not wasted, so that energy reserves will last for as long as possible.

Nuclear power is one alternative that is in use today. It would be possible to increase the amount of this type of energy. At present there are problems of how to dispose of the waste products formed from the reactors. They have to be made perfectly safe!

Fig. 7.4 Energy sources of the future? (*continued opposite*)

Iceland makes use of naturally occurring hot water (Fig. 7.4) from hot-water springs. The hot rock deep in the Earth's crust heats underground stores of water which are then forced to the surface. This is known as **geothermal** energy. It may provide a considerable amount of energy in the future in many places around the world.

France is already making use of the tides to provide an alternative energy source. The Rance Tidal Barrage allows water to flow through it easily in one direction. When the tide turns, the water is made to run back through a series of turbines and generate electricity. Unfortunately, it can only be used at certain times of the day. Because it uses the tides, it has a slowing effect on the rotation of the Earth! (It is very, very small!) It is possible that a similar tidal power station could be built in the Bristol Channel.

In America and the United Kingdom large experimental windmills (aero-generators) are being used to produce electricity (see Fig. 7.4). They need to be built in places that are very windy for much of the year if they are to be of use for producing electricity. Many of these places are considered to be areas of outstanding natural beauty! Using the wind is not new. Holland, for example, has been using wind power for hundreds of years. (There are 950 surviving windmills!)

Solar power is almost unlimited. Watches and calculators that run on solar cells are very common. Collecting the sun's energy (see Fig. 7.4) on a large scale is a much more difficult task. Certain parts of the world are much more suitable for solar power stations than others. The hotter lands nearer the equator are much better placed to use this energy source. There is a solar power station now being tested in France.

Activities

1 Coal and coke are 'old' fuels – see Sections 7.3 and 7.4. Look at a small piece of coal under a magnifying glass. Now look at a piece of coke under the magnifying glass. There are several differences between them, but what are they? Can you compare them to a piece of 'modern' fuel, such as wood? Very carefully try and break the piece of coal. You may be lucky to see some of the layers that were laid down millions of years ago.

> **Warning: these next activities need the use of matches/flames, and you should make sure that you have proper permission to do them – safely! Ask an adult to help you.**

2 Here are a set of experiments for you to try. You will need these bits and pieces:
    a small piece of candle
    a peanut or two
    a milk bottle
    a metal spoon that is not needed any more
    an old egg cup (pottery is best, **not plastic**).

(a) Pour a small amount of **cold** water into the milk bottle. In a safe place, put the candle on a flat surface and light it. Hold the milk bottle over the candle so that the flame is nearly touching the bottom of the bottle. There are two things to look out for. What are they? You will have to be very quick to see one of the changes.

(b) The purpose of this simple experiment is to try and show the energy value of a single peanut. Half fill the egg cup with water. Test the temperature of the water with your finger. Put one of the peanuts onto the spoon. Now try and light it with a match! You should find that it burns quite easily. Hold the egg cup carefully over the peanut flame. Watch your fingers. When the peanut has finally burnt out test the temperature of the water again.

    Is there any change? If there is no change can you suggest a reason for this? (You could always try again with some more peanuts!) What do the burnt peanuts now look like? Do they remind you of anything else?

(c) Clean the milk bottle and refill it with water. **Very carefully** light a ring on a gas cooker if you have one (or a bunsen burner at school). Make sure it is on a **very low flame**. Hold the bottom of the milk bottle over the flame (**only for a few seconds**) and watch again as you did with the candle. You are not trying to heat the water!

(d) Each of the simple experiments have some things in common, but what are they? Is there a link between the types of energy that you have been using?

3 Using the energy chart (Table 7.1) can you make an estimate of how many kilojoules of energy you eat in one meal? Try the same estimation for other people in the household.

4 Make a list of as many reasons as you can for the differences in energy intake for a young person and a senior citizen.

5 Mr and Mrs Average and their children Everso and Osow need to consume an average amount of energy every day to stay fit and healthy. They don't know how much this is. Can you find out for them?

6 An open fire used 10 kg of fuel during a cold winter evening.
(a) How much energy went up the chimney if the fuel used was
  (i) coal?
  (ii) anthracite?
(b) Was all the energy really wasted?
(c) If a 50 kg bag of fuel cost £10, how much did it cost to heat the chimney that evening?

7 Ask if you can see some old electricity or gas bills. Look for the way energy is sold. British gas sell energy in megajoules (that is, millions of joules) per cubic metre, but they also use another unit. Can you find out what it is and what it means?

Summary

The Earth's crust contains vast amounts of natural fuels. The known reserves are slowly being used up. Energy conservation is important so that what remains lasts as long as possible. Alternative energy forms such as nuclear, wind, wave and solar power are becoming future possibilities for use on a wide scale.

Unit 8

Solids, liquids and gases

8.1 The very small

A football is quite small. A tennis ball is smaller. A marble is even smaller. A grain of salt or sand is smaller still. If you put a grain of sand next door to a molecule the sand grain would look huge – really huge! Molecules are amongst the smallest things known. They are impossible to see with the eye, no matter how hard you try. If you put 5 000 000 oil molecules side by side they might just stretch to about a centimetre!

8.2 Molecules

A **molecule** is the smallest, complete, piece of 'stuff' you can get. Everything in the world is made up of molecules, including you. It is a good thing that they are so tiny, because we do not have to think of them by themselves. We can think of them in very large bundles, and this makes it much easier.

8.3 Models

Just as you can buy plastic models that look exactly like the real thing, so we can use a model to help us think of molecules. One model could be marbles, another could be steel ball-bearings. You could think of snooker balls as a molecular model. A class of pupils could act as a set of molecules.

8.4 Solids

When the molecules of a material do not have much energy they are able to bunch together very closely. They arrange themselves in neat patterns clinging to the molecules next door. They are fixed in position and cannot change places (see Fig. 8.1 a). All they can do is vibrate a little. Solids do not flow. They keep their shape and their volume.

8.5 Liquids

A molecule in a liquid has a little more energy than it would if it were in a solid. These molecules are able to move about, but they are not free to move anywhere they like. They often stay together in bunches (droplets). If you put a large number of them in a container they arrange themselves into the same shape as the container (see Fig. 8.1 b). Water from a long thin pipe changes its shape when it is poured into a cup! Its volume does not change.

8.6 Gases

Gas molecules have the most energy of all. They are not tied to any of their next-door neighbours. They are completely free to do what they please. If you put some gas molecules into the corner of a container they will very quickly move around and fill it up. They will be further apart in a large container and closer together in a small one. Because they have a lot of energy gas molecules are always bumping and crashing into one another and the sides of the container (see Fig. 8.1 c).

(a)

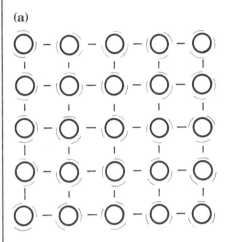

(b)

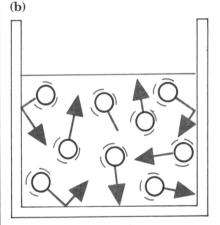

(c)

Fig. 8.1 Solid, liquid or gas?

Activities

1 Imagine you have a cupful of sand and a cupful of marbles. (They can be models of two different kinds of molecules.) What would happen if you were to pour the sand into the cup of marbles? Does this give you an idea of what might happen to two kinds of molecules that are different in size?

2 You will need a kitchen measuring cylinder or jug for this simple experiment. You will also need some methylated spirit and some water.

Warning: methylated spirits is inflammable, so make sure you have permission to try this experiment.

Carefully measure out 50 ml of methylated spirits (meths) and pour it into a cup. Now pour 50 ml of water into the cylinder. Add the 50 ml of meths to the water in the cylinder. The total amount should be 100 ml shouldn't it? What do you notice? From this experiment can you tell anything about the sizes of the two kinds of molecules you have used.

Try this experiment again, but this time dissolve 10 ml of salt into 50 ml of water.

3 Pour a small amount of table salt onto a dark piece of paper and look at it through a magnifying glass. Make sure there is plenty of light. Make a drawing of some of the salt crystals. Are they all different or are there any common shapes? What could this tell you about the molecules in a crystal?

4 The next time you bite into an ice lolly look at the inside. You may well see some ice crystals. If there are any they will be arranged into a pattern. Can you suggest a reason why?

5 Watch the vapour coming from the spout of a boiling kettle. What can you tell about the molecules leaving the spout from just looking at the vapour?

6 This experiment, which is quite easy to do will allow you to try and measure the **size** of a molecule. You will need:
 a clean washing-up bowl full of water
 a ruler
 a small amount of washing-up liquid
 a needle
 some flour
 a calculator
Very carefully sprinkle some flour onto the surface of the water to make a very fine layer. Dip the needle into the washing-up liquid to form a drop on the end (see Fig. 8.2). You have to

Fig. 8.2

measure the width of the drop so it would be sensible to try this several times before going on with the experiment. Record the width (S) in millimetres, of the small drop. Now very gently let the drop fall onto the middle of the water surface. Watch what happens as the drop spreads out. You now have to measure the width (L), in millimetres, of the large circle on the water caused by the washing-up liquid.

The volume of the drop has now been spread evenly over the surface of the water to form a very thin layer. This layer will be roughly one molecule thick. You can use a formula to work out the thickness (that is, the size) of one molecule:

$$\text{thickness of one molecule} = \frac{2 \times S \times S \times S}{3 \times L \times L} \text{ mm}$$

Example. Suppose $S = 2$ mm and $L = 300$ mm.

$$\text{Thickness of one molecule} = \frac{2 \times 2 \times 2 \times 2}{3 \times 300 \times 300} \text{ mm}$$

$$= \frac{16}{270\,000} \text{ mm}$$

$$= 0.000\,059 \text{ mm}$$

Summary

Molecules in a solid are fixed and cannot move. All they can do is shake or vibrate in their place. Molecules in a liquid can move but they are not free, like the molecules in a gas.

Unit 9

Surface tension and capillary action

9.1 Liquid skins

There are many tiny insects that seem to skate or move on top of water. It is almost as if there is a skin on the surface where the water meets the air. The pond skater, the whirlygig beetle and the mosquito larva all use this stretchy skin to support themselves (see Fig. 9.1 a). If they were to break this skin they would sink. This effect of a liquid's surface is known as **surface tension**. It is not really a skin, though. It is an effect caused by the molecules in the water. All liquids have a surface tension, but some are stronger than others.

Surface tension makes drips from a tap into spheres and soap bubbles perfectly round.

9.2 Capillary action

This is another effect caused by the molecules in a liquid. Many liquids can be drawn into small gaps by **capillary action**. Water, for example, seems to creep up inside a thin straw. It also appears to cling to the side of a glass or cup. Water from the ground seeps up through bricks making them damp. House walls are made with a damp-proof course (Fig. 9.1 b) to stop this. One good use for capillary action is in a baby's nappy!

Fig. 9.1
(a) Surface tension at work.
(b) A damp-proof course in a house.

Unit 9  continued

9.3 Cohesion and adhesion

Both surface tension and capillary action are caused by attraction between molecules. Molecules are naturally attracted to other molecules (Fig. 8.1). When molecules are attracted to their own kind it is called **cohesion**. If molecules are attracted to different kinds of molecules, then it is called **adhesion**.

When water is poured out of a glass beaker there are drops left behind clinging to the glass. This happens because of the adhesion of the water molecules to the glass molecules.

An upward curving surface or meniscus is formed when water meets a glass surface. (Water molecules are attracted more to glass molecules than to other water molecules!) If mercury were used instead then the meniscus would curve downwards (see Fig. 9.2). Mercury is more attracted to itself than to glass.

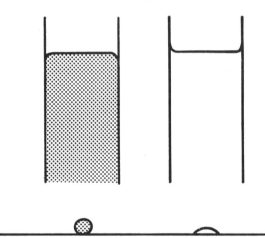

Fig. 9.2 Which is water, which is mercury?

9.4 Wetting surfaces

What happens when water is spilt on a bench? The bench becomes **wet**. This is because the adhesion force (the attraction of a water molecule for one of the molecules in the bench) is greater than the cohesion force (the attraction of a water molecule for another water molecule). Mercury molecules prefer themselves to any other kind. They usually form small drops on their own. Water will wet many surfaces; mercury will not wet any!

9.5 Wetting agents and waterproofing

Soaps and detergents are examples of wetting agents. They help reduce surface tension so that objects become 'wetter' more easily.

Oil is one material that will help keep water out. Birds use natural oil on their feathers to keep the water out so they float. Creosote is use to stop water from entering porous wood.

Activities

1 Glues are often called 'adhesives'; can you suggest a reason why?

2 Look very carefully at the drops formed by a dripping tap. What shape are they just before they fall? Does this shape change at all?

3 Half fill a clear glass with water. Pour into this a few drops of cooking oil. Observe the shape of the oil on the water surface. Slowly pour into the glass some methylated spirit. As the meths and water mix, the oil drops should begin to change shape. What shape do they become? What causes this?

4 For this easy experiment you will need:
a flat, non-porous surface (a kitchen work surface is ideal)
a few drops of oil
some washing-up liquid
a little water
On the work surface, close to the edge, place a few drops of oil. With your finger spread the oil into a circle about 10 cm across. Place two or three drops of water on to the centre of the circle. At the same time place a similar amount of water on to the work surface nearby. Watch the two patches of water change shape. Make a drawing of them looking at them from the edge of the work surface. Are they the same shape? Put a tiny amount of washing-up liquid on the end of a spoon. Watch very closely as you dab the end of the spoon, first on to the plain water patch and then on to the water on top of the oil. Make a second drawing of the water patches now and compare them. Do not forget to clear up!

5 From an old coat hanger make a wire loop about 10 cm across (Fig. 9.3). Practice dipping the loop into some washing-up solution so that a film of soap forms across it. Try making some large bubbles. With a soap film on the loop hold it horizontally. Look at the film. Hold the loop above the washing-up solution and pour some drops of the liquid on to the surface of the film in the wire loop. Watch as the drops go right through the film. Why does the film not break?

6 There are many simple experiments you can try with the film loop you have just made. Tie a piece of cotton across the loop (not tight!). Now dip it in the soap solution. Using this as a starting point what experiments can you make up?

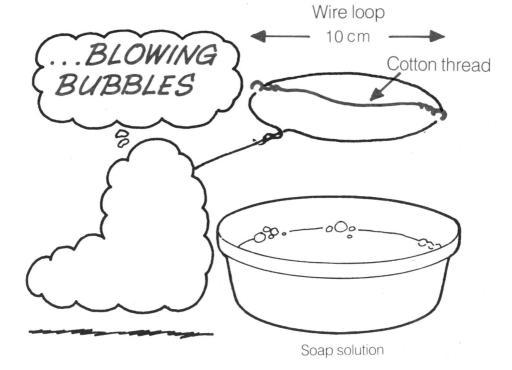

Fig. 9.3

Soap solution

7 It is possible to make a steel paper clip float on water! You will need a glass full of water and quite a few paper clips. You might have to change the shape of the paper clip to succeed. (The sharper ends sometimes pierce the water surface!) Don't give up if it doesn't work first time!

8 Cut off a 4 cm wide strip of any kind of paper hanky or kitchen roll. About 2 cm from one end write your name across the strip. Hold the other end of the strip. Slowly lower the end nearest your name so that it just touches the surface of some water. Watch! What do you see? Why does this happen?

Fig. 9.4

9 Place an empty glass on a table top. Fill another glass with water and place it next to the empty glass, but raised up about 5 cm above the table top. Use a single strand of wool about 15 cm long and dip one end into the glass of water. Drape the other end into the empty glass (Fig. 9.4). Leave the experiment for about an hour. When you return can you explain what has occurred by thinking about the molecules of the water and wool?

10 Look around the outside of some nearby houses. Can you find their damp-proof courses?

11 What do you see when you:
(a) 'dunk' a biscuit in tea or coffee?
(b) have a shower curtain made of a 'cloth' material and it is sprayed with water?

Summary

Surface tension and capillary action effects are caused by molecules acting on one another.

Unit 10

Naming forces

10.1 Forces all around us

No matter where you go there are forces at work all around you. *Forces* are pushes or pulls. Forces cause things to move or turn or stay still (Fig. 10.1). Sometimes forces are given special names that almost hide their real meaning.

10.2 Naming forces

Friction This is a force between two objects in contact. It can be useful when we want to stop something and a nuisance when we want to start or keep something moving. Friction in liquids is called **viscosity**.

Resistance or **drag** This is also a force that opposes motion. The drag of the air resistance of a car increases with speed.

Tension A stretched spring or rope has a force pulling at both ends (Fig. 10.2). This tension has to be equal at each end. It would look very strange if a rope were tight at one end and slack at the other.

Fig. 10.2

Fig. 10.1 Natural forces at work

Upthrust When you go swimming the water helps to support you so that you don't sink. It helps to keep you buoyant. This is an 'upthrust' force.

Expansion An example of this would be the force of water expanding when it freezes, causing pipes to burst. Iron railway lines may have gaps in them to make room for expansion to stop them bending and buckling. The force of expansion by materials such as iron is very strong.

Magnetism This is an invisible force that can be very strong too. A compass is an example of a magnetic force at work.

Electric These forces can make your hair cling to a plastic comb or your clothes stick together. (Balloons can be 'stuck' to the walls at party time using electric forces.)

Gravity This is one of the most important forces of all. The Earth pulls everything towards it with the force of gravity. The Moon has a gravity too.

10.3 Forces in action

Forces can:

speed things up	squash things
slow things down	cause bending
prevent movement	turn objects
make objects change	twist objects
direction	cause distortion
stretch things	

Activities

1 Can you suggest how 'a Dragster' (Fig. 10.3) might have come by its name? or why one brand of engine oil is called 'BP Viscostatic'?

2 From a roll of 'cling film' cut off a strip about 15 cm long and 3 cm wide (any other strip of plastic will do). Grip both ends tightly and try to pull them apart. The idea is to stretch the film very slowly but not to break it! Look for any changes in the film.

3 You will need a pair of Polaroid sunglasses and the clear plastic portion of a tape cassette case for this simple experiment. Use the plastic case to reflect the light from a bright lamp. Look at the reflections through the sunglasses. You should be able to see a variety of colours. These are caused by the forces that were trapped inside the plastic when it was formed. Now gently start twisting the case. What do you see now? Can you explain these new observations? Through the sunglasses look at other materials in the same way. Do they produce colours too?

4 Fig. 10.4 shows some forces in action (they are shown by the arrows). Study each of them and then decide:
 (i) which object the force is working on;
 (ii) if the force is a push or pull;
 (iii) the name or cause of the force;
 (iv) the effect the force has.

Fig. 10.3

Activities continued

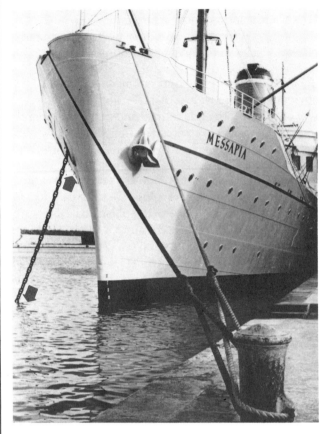

Fig. 10.4
above:
(a) *(right)*
(b) *(left)*
below:
(c) *(right)*
(d) *(left)*

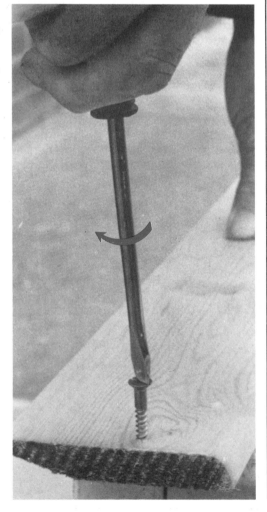

Summary

Forces involve pushes or pulls. They are all around us and we could not exist without them. They have many different names that sometimes hide them so that they don't seem like forces at all.

Unit 11

Measuring forces

11.1 Units of force

We have met several units of measurement up to now. Forces have units, too, and they are measured in **newtons** (N). If you hold four ordinary bags of crisps they will be pressing down with a force of just over one newton (1 N), so you see it is quite a small force (see Fig. 11.1).

Fig. 11.1 What are these 'forces' worth?

A family-sized bag of sugar (1 kg) placed on a table pushes downwards with a force of only 10 newtons (10 N).

11.2 Measuring forces

We can use the pulling, pushing and bending effects of forces to make measuring devices (Fig. 11.2). The more a spring is pulled the more it stretches. This idea is used in a newton-meter. They are very common and you will probably have some at school. Springs can also be compressed or squashed, and so they too can be used to measure forces.

If you have used a bottle opener or tried to open a tin with a lever you know that a force is needed. If you use too much force, the opener or lever may bend or break. Just as a spring can be made to stretch, so a lever or bar can be made to bend.

Fig. 11.2 What are these, and what do they do?
(*continued next page*)

Unit 11 continued

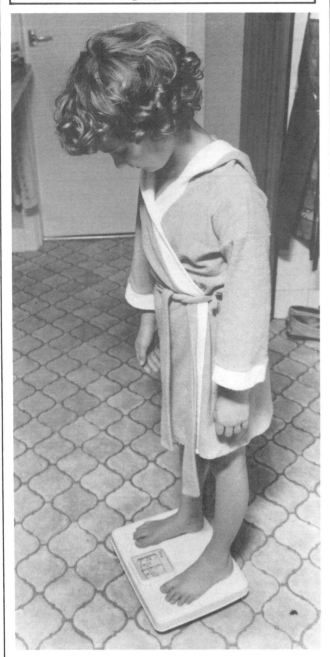

Fig. 11.2 (*continued*)

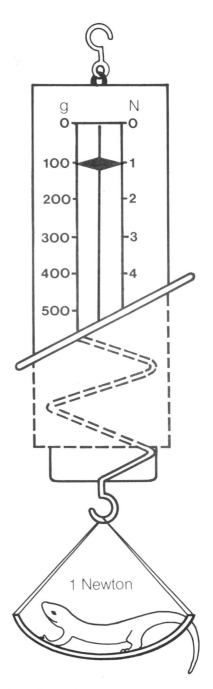

Fig. 11.3 A newton-meter

A common garage tool is a torque-wrench. This is made so that the handle bends a little, and as it bends a scale shows you how much force is being used. This is very useful for making sure that nuts and bolts are tightened correctly. It could be disastrous if they started to work loose!

11.3 The newton-meter

Some newton-meters (like the one in Fig. 11.3) are marked with two separate scales. In Fig. 11.3 the second scale is marked off in grams (g). Force [measured in newtons (N)] and mass [measured in grams (g) or kilograms (kg)] are linked, **but** they are not the same. We will see how they are linked later on!

Activities

1 Can you find out more about the torque-wrench?

2 You will probably find some 'force measurers' at home, BUT they may seem to be called different names. How many can you find? If they are not labelled in newtons, how are they labelled? How hard can you push/pull?

3 Match the force values (of something pushing down onto the ground) with the correct object:

Force (N)	Object
1 N	A 5-litre can of petrol
50 N	The Guinness Book of Records
350 N	An apple
10 N	You!

4 PHYSICS IN HISTORY Read this and then answer the questions that follow.

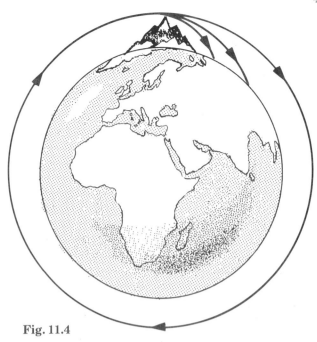

Fig. 11.4

Sir Isaac Newton

In 1642 Galileo died. In the same year Isaac Newton was born. He was the son of a Lincolnshire farmer. As a young child he was quite sickly and very shy. He went to the King's School, Grantham. After four years, as he had shown little progress, his mother took him away in order to let him become a farmer. Farming was not to prove the ideal occupation. Isaac's uncle persuaded his mother to change her mind and let him return to school. After a fight with a school bully a new confidence came over him, and he finally went on to University to study at Trinity College, Cambridge.

As a boy he was fond of making things. He made a wooden windmill (that was driven by mouse-power), waterclocks and sundials. This practical experience was of great use to him later on, as he had to make much of his experimental apparatus.

The university was closed in 1665 for two years because of the plague. Isaac used this 'spare time' for private study during which he laid the foundations for many of his future discoveries. He was not yet 25. When he was 27 he was made Professor of Mathematics at Cambridge! One of his most important discoveries was announced in 1684 when he proposed his theory of gravitation. Today Newton is considered to have been one of the world's greatest men of science.

He once suggested a 'thought experiment'. He imagined a very tall mountain from which he could fire a bullet. The idea was that if he fired it fast enough it would circle the Earth as it fell and would eventually return to the starting place (see Fig. 11.4).

In addition to all of his great scientific work he also applied himself to simple everyday problems. He is said to have cut a hole in the doorway so that the cat could enter and leave on its own. When the cat had kittens he made some smaller holes; one for each of them! Perhaps this was the earliest 'cat-flap'?

(a) Suggest one reason why Newton might not have enjoyed being a farmer?
(b) How did one of the skills he acquired when he was young help him in later life?
(c) How old was he when he put forward the idea of 'gravity'?
(d) Using the idea of the 'bullet' can you think of any other practical examples of the same idea?

Activities continued

Fig. 11.5 Sir Isaac Newton

Brainteasers: you may need the help of a library with the next three questions.

(e) What do Newton, Galileo and the Leaning Tower of Pisa have in common?

(f) Newton and Galileo share something else in common and they both have one named after them. What is the link?

(g) In addition to his work on forces, Newton made many other fascinating and colourful discoveries. You can try some of them out at home, but you will have to find out what they are first!

Summary

Forces are most easily measured using a newton-meter. They are named after Sir Isaac Newton. Weighing machines are not really well named unless they are marked with the units of force – newtons.

Unit 12

Passing on forces

12.1 Using forces

As you know, forces can be useful. If you want to stop a bike, then you need to apply a force to slow you down. The easiest way is to put on the brakes. The brakes themselves are some way away from the handlebars, and so it is necessary to find a way to pass on (or transfer) the braking force easily from the handlebars to the brakes.

12.2 Passing on forces

One of the simpler ways of passing a force on is to use a rod, rope or spring. The force is transferred from one end to the other. Exactly the same force is passed on if two or more springs/ropes are joined end to end. The same is not so if they are arranged like those of the car in Fig. 12.1. In this example there are four separate springs holding it up. Because they are separate they each take a share in supporting the car. The force pushing down onto the ground has been passed on by the four springs.

Gravity provides you with a downwards force. The arches of your feet pass this force onto the ground using the sole and the heel.

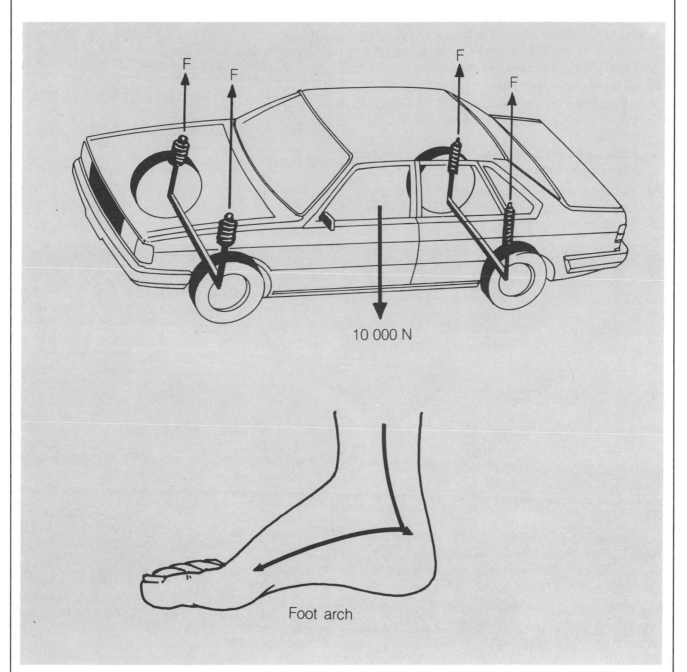

10 000 N

Foot arch

Fig. 12.1

Unit 12 continued

12.3 Using fluids

It is quite easy to pass on a force, but springs and things are not always easy to use. Fluids flow, and so they should be much easier to direct to where they are needed. Gases and liquids both flow very easily, but which is best?

In Unit 8 we met molecules from liquids and gases. The gas molecules were surrounded by a lot of spare space. Gases can be compressed easily. Liquid molecules are closely packed and cannot be compressed. Liquids are better at passing on forces. You may have seen the equipment shown in Fig. 12.2 at school. This is used to investigate how good fluids are at transmitting forces.

12.4 The bicycle

This very simple machine uses the idea of passing on forces in many different ways. It also illustrates very well that physics is all around us.

(a) The force of the rider pushing downwards is transmitted through the wheels to the ground.
(b) The handlebars transmit a turning force to the front wheel.
(c) Braking, you hope, is done by a force passed on by the brake cable.
(d) To keep the machine in motion, the driving force is transmitted from the pedals to the rear wheel by a chain.

Fig. 12.2 (b) Passing on forces

Fig. 12.2 (a) Passing on forces

Activities

1 The apparatus shown in Fig. 12.2 is very easy to use. You could make a similar arrangement (with a bicycle pump perhaps?) and try the experiment for yourself! Make a list of 10 separate sentences describing the way in which you would carry out this experiment. Take great care when putting the sentences in order.

2 See if you can obtain any old pumps and ask if you can take them apart. A bicycle pump is again useful for this because it should go back together very easily! What are the names of the various parts and what do they do? Make a carefully labelled drawing of a pump you have taken apart!

3 How many different shapes and styles of bridge can you find? Make up a photo-collection.

4 What do your feet and the Eiffel Tower have in common?

5 Find a spider's web, and by touching it carefully look to see how it transmits forces. For their size the webs are very strong. Why might this be?

6 Building bridges. For this simple experiment you will need the following bits and pieces:
two supports (such as bricks or thick books)
several small stones (about the same size as one another)
several sheets of writing paper
The idea is to construct a bridge from paper, lay it between the two supports and then test it to see how good it is at passing on forces. (That is, in passing the weight of the stones to the supports.) The better the design, the better the bridge will be at passing on the forces to the supports. Use a new piece of paper each time you build a new bridge. Some ideas for bridges are shown in Fig. 12.3.

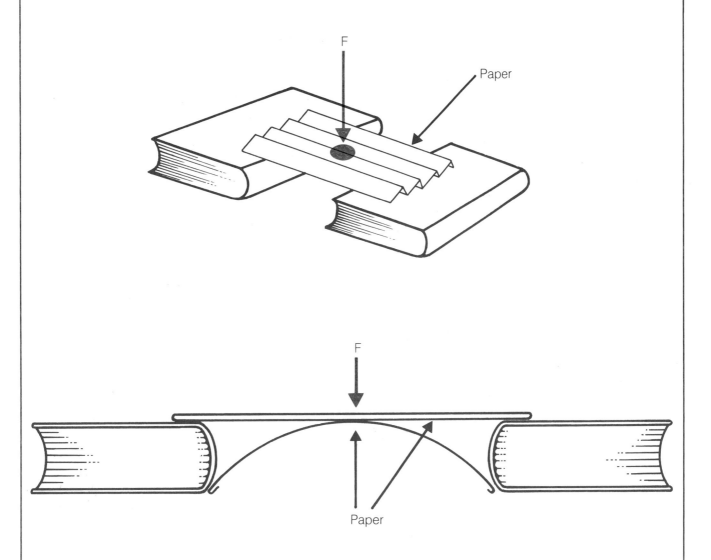

Fig. 12.3 Building bridges

Activities continued

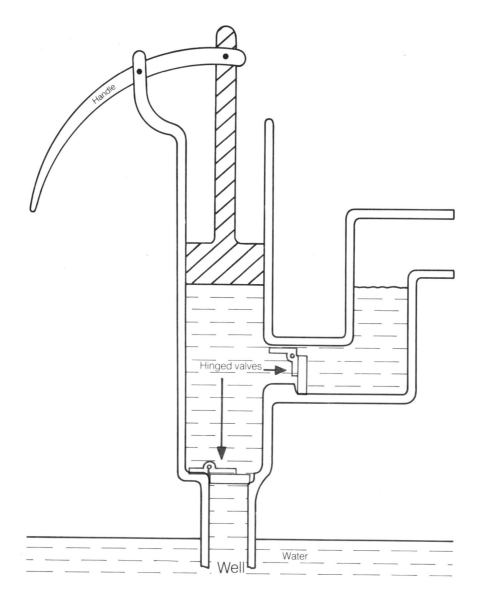

Fig. 12.4 The force pump

Brainteasers

7 Cars use special oils in their braking systems. Can you find a diagram or drawing showing how they work? Why is it important not to get air bubbles in the brake pipes?

8 Look at Fig. 12.4. This is an illustration of a 'force pump' and it is used to raise water from a well. It is simply made with a handle, a piston and two valves.

To raise water the handle is first moved up and then down. There are several places in the pump where forces are transmitted. How many can you find? How does the pump work?

9 When you ride a bicycle hard why is the chain often tight along the top edge and slack along the bottom? Shouldn't the tension be the same all the way round (like an elastic band)?

Summary

Forces can be transmitted in many different ways, but one of the most effective is by using a liquid. Liquids are chosen because they cannot be compressed, and they can be made to transmit forces in any direction easily.

Unit 13

Pairs of forces

13.1 More than one force

As you will have seen by now, forces don't appear on their own. Newton was the first to notice that they always come in pairs and that a single force is an impossibility.

13.2 Gravity and you

Wherever you are or whatever you are doing, gravity is acting on you. It is always providing you with a downwards force. Forces cause things to happen and yet nothing happens to you! Strange as it may seem the Earth is pushing back on you with a force equal to that of gravity! The result is that you go nowhere. The forces are balanced. In just the same way when you sit down on a stool or chair it pushes up on you with a force of the same size.

13.3 Action and reaction

Imagine you are leaning against a tree. You are acting (providing a force by leaning) on the tree and it reacts against you (by stopping you). Your push is called the **action force** and the force of the tree against you is called the **reaction force**.

Jumping to shore from a small boat (see Fig. 13.1) can prove disastrous because action–reaction forces are at work. As you try and jump one way, the boat will move in the opposite direction. It could dampen your spirits!

Another simple example of an action–reaction pair of forces is 'walking'. When you take a step forward you exert a backwards force on the ground (action) and it very conveniently provides a forward force (reaction) on you. The result is that you move forward and the Earth moves backward! Because the Earth is so massive, it hardly notices the difference.

An action–reaction pair of forces always acts on a pair of objects. They cannot work on the same object.

Fig. 13.1 Action – reaction pairs

Unit 13 continued

Fig. 13.2 What causes lift-off?

13.4 Unbalanced forces

So far, the pairs of forces have been balanced. They have been of equal size, but in opposite directions, and so in effect they cancel one another out. If one of the pair of forces were much larger than the other then it would have a greater effect.

When the engines of a space rocket ignite they provide a force acting against gravity. While this force is small the rocket will stay still. When the force has increased to the same value as that of gravity the rocket will be just able to support itself (hover?). When the exhaust gases can provide a force greater than that of gravity the rocket will begin to rise from the launch pad and start to gather speed. When in space the rocket still has something to push against – the exhaust gases.

13.5 Resultant forces

In Fig. 13.2 two forces are in use, in opposite directions. One is larger than the other. The difference between the two of them is known as a **resultant**. It is the resultant force that causes a rocket to rise against gravity.

Activities

1 Challenge someone to a game of Blow Football (you could make it from straws and a paper ball!). It demonstrates a pair of forces acting on an object. If one of the players has more 'puff' than the other then the resulting force will control the direction and speed of the ball.

2 These next two experiments will need the use of some bathroom scales and the help of a friend.

(a) Hold the scales in front of you and squeeze them as hard as you can. What are the forces being used? Can you identify an action – reaction pair?

Fig. 13.3

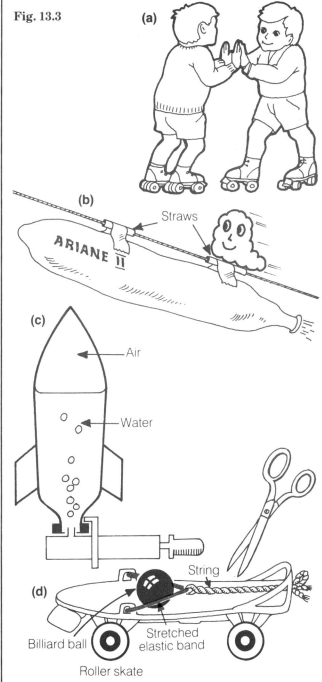

Fig. 13.4 How does the spaceman get about?

(c) If you can use one of the rockets shown, in Fig. 13.3 (c), **read the rocket's instructions carefully and only use it outside**.

(d) Try the experiment shown in Fig. 13.3 d on a flat surface out of doors.

4 What do you think is the purpose of the backpack the spaceman is wearing (Fig. 13.4), and how does it work?

Brainteaser

5 With your portable tool-kit you have been making repairs to the outside of a spacecraft when you lose your grip. As you float away you can see the spacecraft on your left. It is not very far away but it is out of reach. How do you return to safety?

(b) Put the scales on the floor, stand on them and crouch down. The idea is to jump up very quickly and see if there is any change of the scale value. You are looking for a change that occurs immediately you begin to jump upwards. What change is there? Can you explain this observation with the help of action–reaction forces?

3 Look at Fig. 13.3, which shows a selection of experiments that involve a pair of forces. Can you spot the forces? Are there any action–reaction pairs?

(a) In Fig. 13.3 a, one person pushes/both push but who moves?

(b) Blow up the balloon and let it travel along the thread (Fig. 13.3 b).

Summary

Forces always act in pairs. An action–reaction pair of forces are always equal and opposite. When two or more pairs of forces combine they form a resultant (which can be zero).

Unit 14

Measuring temperature

14.1 Hot and cold

It is very difficult to explain to someone what hotness or coldness is. What may feel hot to one person may feel cold to another. Even if it is possible to given an idea of hot and cold how do you explain 'warm'? We need to have a definite scale of hotness and coldness. This scale is called **temperature**.

Fig. 14.1 is a diagram that shows a selection of hot and cold temperatures, in order; hottest at the top and coldest at the bottom. To say if something is hot or cold depends on where you are on the scale to start with. Looking upwards, 'Mumbles' sees hot things and looking downwards sees cold things. If standing somewhere else on the scale, 'Mumbles' would think differently about what was hot and what was cold.

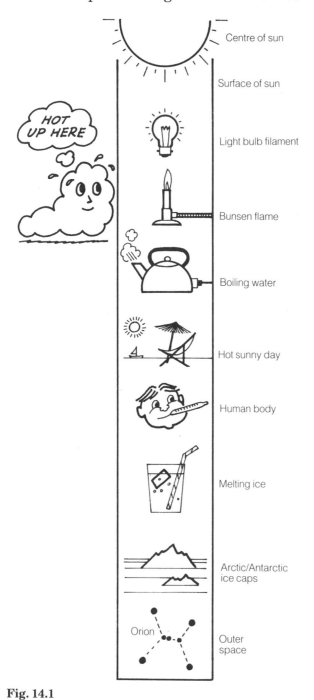

Fig. 14.1

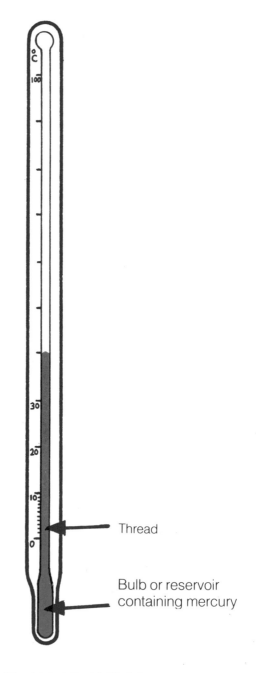

Fig. 14.2 A liquid-filled thermometer

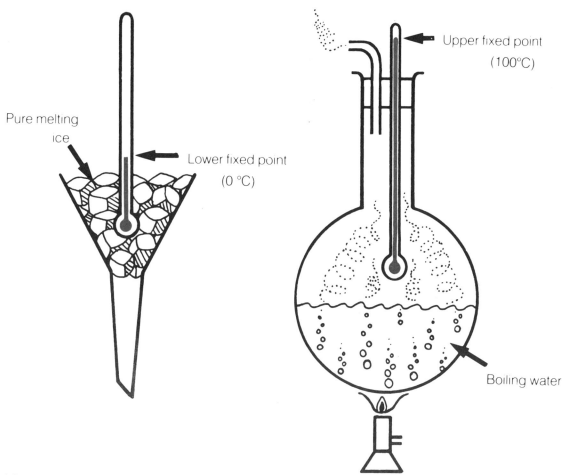

Fig. 14.3

14.2 Temperature scales

There are two temperature scales in use: **celsius** (C), commonly called **Centigrade**, and the less-well-known **Kelvin** (K) scale. The Centigrade scale is split into 100 equal divisions or **degrees** (°C) (Fig. 14.2).

The zero mark (0 °C) on this scale is the temperature of pure, melting ice. The 100 (100 °C) mark is the temperature of the steam above pure boiling water. These are known as fixed points. Methods of finding them are shown in Fig. 14.3.

14.3 Centigrade and Kelvin conversions

To change a temperature from Celsius (Centigrade) to Kelvin simply **add** 273. To change a temperature from Kelvin to Celsius (Centigrade), **subtract** 273. For example:

400 °C = 673K
250° C = 523K
373K = 100 °C
173K = −100 °C

Activities

1 You are going to plot a graph and then answer the questions that follow. The graph in Fig. 14.4 has been set out to convert Centigrade (°C) into Fahrenheit (°F). (This is an old temperature scale that appears occasionally.) Copy the graph onto a piece of graph paper and fill in any missing labels/numbers, etc. Use the x-axis for Centigrade and the y-axis for Fahrenheit. You are going to use the information in the boxes to plot the graph. The first point has been plotted for you.

Activities continued

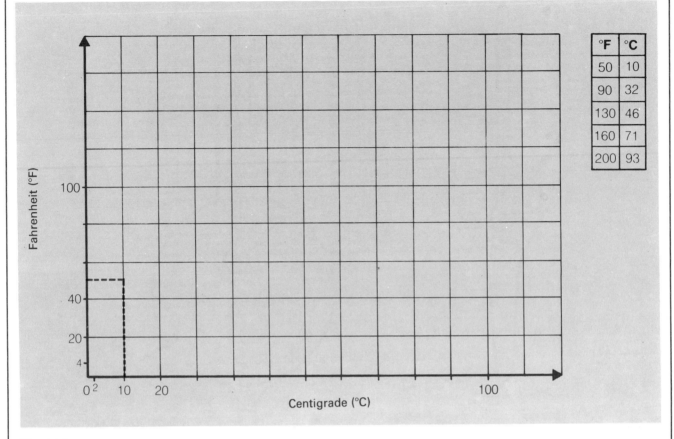

°F	°C
50	10
90	32
130	46
160	71
200	93

Fig. 14.4

Your graph should follow a more or less straight path. Use a ruler to draw a single straight line through as many of the points as you can.

(a) Are there any points that seem really out of place?

(b) What are the temperatures in °F of ice and steam?

(c) Find the missing temperature conversions:

°C	°F
?	0
−10	?
?	100
60	?
?	220

2 Match the following temperatures with the most likely event:

°C	Event
1530	Room temperature
19	Body temperature
37	Melting point of iron
600	Liquid nitrogen
−196	Open fire

Brainteaser. You may need the use of a library for this next question.

3 'Fahrenheit 451' is the title of a science fiction book by Ray Bradbury. What is the importance of 451 °F? What are the equivalent Celsius (Centigrade) and Kelvin temperatures?

Summary

Temperature is a measure of hotness and coldness. It is not a measure of heat energy. The two scales in common use are Celsius (Centigrade) and Kelvin.

Unit 15

Thermometers

15.1 Temperature and change

If we want to find an easy way to measure temperature, then we have to find a quantity that changes as that material becomes hotter or colder.

A simple example of this idea would be the use of colour. An iron poker left in a fire gradually turns red as it increases in temperature. The colour change will continue on to orange then yellow and finally white. As it cools the colours slowly change back again.

There are many changes to choose from, but the most commonly used, for everyday thermometers, are changes in colour or volume. As computers and control technology become more and more important, it is very useful to have thermometers that work by causing changes in the flow of electricity.

15.2 Liquid-in-glass thermometers

These work on the principle that most liquids increase in volume when they are heated. The liquid is held in a reservoir at the base of the thermometer. When the temperature increases, the liquid expands and rises up the thin tube next to the scale. If the tube is made very thin, then the thermometer will be more sensitive to temperature changes.

15.3 The mercury thermometer

These are hazardous if they are broken, especially as mercury and mercury vapour are poisonous. The thread is easy to see and mercury doesn't 'wet' the sides of the tube. Mercury reacts quickly to changes in temperature, but it freezes at $-39\,°C$ and so it is not suitable for Arctic conditions. Mercury boils at $360\,°C$.

15.4 The alcohol thermometer

Alcohol is colourless and needs to have a dye added to make it easily seen. It 'wets' glass and the thread sometimes breaks. Alcohol is an inexpensive liquid that boils at $78\,°C$ and freezes at $-112\,°C$. It expands more than mercury, and so a wider tube can be used, but it is slower to react to temperature change.

15.5 The clinical thermometer

The clinical thermometer is a special variety of mercury thermometer. As the temperature of the human body only ranges over a few degrees, so too does the clinical thermometer. It has to be very accurate and so the mercury tube has to be very thin. The average body temperature is $36.9\,°C$. Fig. 15.1 shows a clinical thermometer with a very special 'kink' or constriction in the tube. As the thermometer is removed from the patient's mouth the temperature reading will begin to fall. The kink prevents this by causing the mercury thread to break, leaving the thermometer registering the patient's maximum temperature.

15.6 Thermometers in industry

Resistance thermometers rely on the fact that it becomes more and more difficult to pass electricity through a material the hotter it becomes. They can be used to measure temperatures from about $-200\,°C$ to $1200\,°C$. Fig. 15.2 shows some examples.

Thermocouple thermometers are made from two wires of different materials joined together. When they become hot an electric current flows. They work over a temperature range $-200\,°C$ to $1600\,°C$.

Pyrometers use colour changes to register changes in temperatures. They can quite easily be used to measure furnace temperatures up to a few thousand degrees.

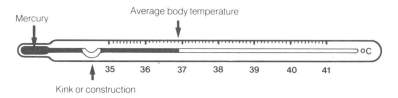

Fig. 15.1 A clinical thermometer

Unit 15 continued

Fig. 15.2 What are these called, and what use are they?

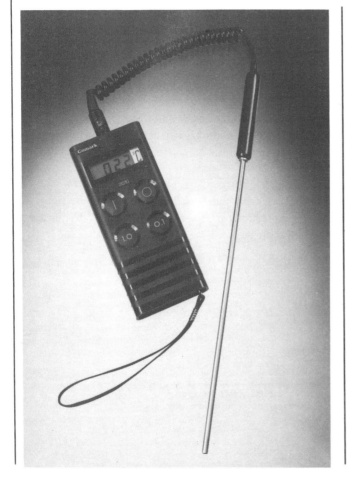

Activities

1 Half-fill a deep dish or saucepan with cold water. Half-fill a second with warm water and then half-fill a third with hot water, but not too hot (see Fig. 15.3). Place one hand in the cold water and the other in the hot water. Leave them in the water for one minute. Now place both hands in the warm water. What does this tell you about temperature? Would you make a good thermometer?

2 Make a list of the advantages and disadvantages of mercury and alcohol thermometers. Compare the lists you have made.

Fig. 15.3

3 Why do nurses and doctors always shake clinical thermometers before use? Why would it not be sensible to sterilize one of these in boiling water? How are they sterilized?

4 Ask if you can borrow a clinical thermometer for this simple experiment. First of all make sure that you can read the scale on the thermometer. Put it in your mouth, under your tongue. Leave it there for two minutes. Take your temperature reading. Repeat this several times during a day or every day for a week. Record all of your readings and at the end of the experiment look back at all the 'data' (the bits of information) you have collected. On a piece of graph paper make a bar chart or block graph. This will show your results well.

(a) Are there any changes?

(b) Do any patterns appear?

(c) Could you add to this graph another set of results from someone else?

5 What is thermostat and how did it get its name?

6 Six had a thermometer named after him – Six's Maximum and Minimum Thermometer. Can you find out more about him and his thermometer?

7 How many different household items can you find that need some kind of temperature control to make them operate properly?

Brainteasers

8 Elizabeth bought the last mercury-in-glass thermometer (range: 0 °C to 100 °C) in a sale. When she arrived home she found that all the markings had rubbed off though the thermometer still worked (Fig. 15.4). She remembered reading a book – 'Foundation Skills Physics'. Without getting any hotter under her collar she immediately set to work re-marking the thermometer. How did she do it?

Fig. 15.4 How do you find the temperature value?

9 Philip (Elizabeth's know-all brother), decided to try and use the thermometer to measure the temperature inside their freezer. After a little while he announced a temperature of −10 °C. How could he know that?

Summary

There are many types of thermometer for domestic and industrial use. It is important to use the thermometer that is right for the temperature range to be measured.

Unit 16

Heating and cooling

16.1 The three states

Materials exist in three distinct ways. Each of these three is known as a **state**: they are solid, liquid and gas. Most materials can be made to exist in all three states (see Fig. 16.1). The substance we know as water is in the liquid state. When it freezes it changes into the solid state (ice) and when it boils it changes into the gaseous state (steam).

WHAT A STATE I'M IN

Sauna

Fig. 16.1

16.2 Changing state

Heat energy is responsible for changing the state of a material. Adding heat can change a solid into a liquid and a liquid into a gas. Taking heat away from a substance has the reverse effect. To understand why materials change state we need to go back to the idea of molecules that we met in Unit 8.

In order to turn a solid into a liquid, the arrangement of molecules will have to be changed. In a solid they are all neatly and tightly bound together. In a liquid they are able to move around. We need to find a way to pull the molecules apart from one another. To do this energy is needed. One of the most convenient forms is heat. As heat is supplied to the solid the vibrations of the molecules increase. The vibrations become so violent that the molecules begin to separate. The solid is changing to a liquid. Even with their new energy, the molecules are still attracted to one another, but they can now move around.

For the change from a liquid to a gas more energy must be given to the molecules. They need enough energy to break away from their neighbours completely. They will then be free to move where they want to.

This idea of molecular movement leads us to think more about the meaning of heat energy. Remember, moving energy is given the name 'kinetic energy', so it must be very closely linked to what we call heat.

16.3 Latent heat

Normally, when something is heated, the temperature will just go on rising. When the state of a material is about to change, then all the heat supplied is needed to make the state change. During this time the temperature does not go up or down. When the change of state has been completed, the temperature can start to rise again. Heat energy is added during the change, but you do not notice this as there is no visible effect on a thermometer. The heat energy has been 'hidden'. This hidden heat is called **latent heat**.

16.4 Melting or freezing?

The following words are used to describe changes of state.

By adding heat: a solid **melts** to become a liquid and then **vaporizes** into a gas.

By removing heat: a gas **condenses** into a liquid and then **freezes** (**fuses** together) to become solid.

These changes are shown in Fig. 16.2.

Fig. 16.2

The heat needed to cause the change of a solid to and from a liquid is known as the **latent heat of fusion**. This change takes place only at the **melting point**.

The heat needed to cause the change to and from a gas is known as the **latent heat of vaporization**. This takes place only at the **boiling point**.

Similarly, when a hot liquid is cooled, it gives out heat, and the temperature falls. When the liquid begins to go solid, the temperature doesn't fall any more, but heat is still given out. When all the liquid has solidified, the temperature carries on falling.

The temperature at which the liquid begins to solidify is called the **freezing point**.

If you start to heat the solid, it will melt at the freezing point. The freezing point of a hot liquid cooling is the same as the melting point of the solid being heated (see Fig. 16.3).

16.5 Units of specific latent heat

When 1 kg of ice is at its melting point it needs an extra 334 000 J of energy to turn it into water (2 kg of ice will need 2 × 334 000 J). This extra energy is the **specific latent heat of fusion**. It is the energy needed to melt completely 1 kg of a material. The units are joules per kilogram (J/kg).

The value of the specific latent heat of water (into steam) is 2 260 000 J/kg. It is because this value is so high that steam scalds badly. You absorb all the energy that is given out when the steam condenses! Table 16.1 shows a selection of specific latent heat values. Some of these are very large.

16.6 Warming things up

Luckily, most materials exist in a steady state. They remain a solid or a liquid or a gas. It is necessary to give them energy to raise their

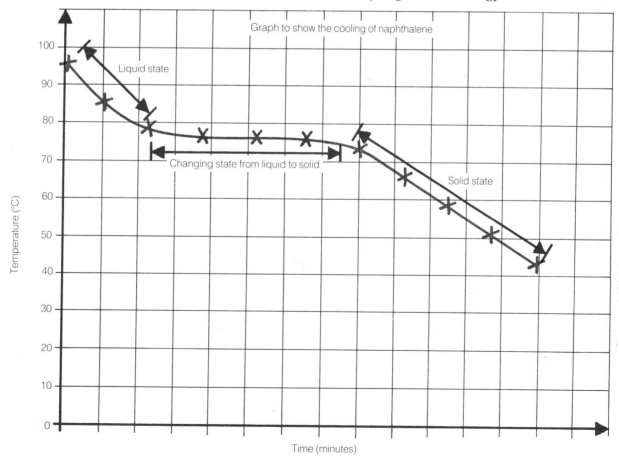

Fig. 16.3 What is the freezing/melting point of naphthalene shown by this cooling curve?

Unit 16 continued

Fusion		Vaporization	
Ice	334 000	Water	2 260 000
Lead	24 700	—	
Gold	66 000	—	
—		Ether	377 000
Mercury	12 000	Mercury	301 000

Table 16.1 Latent heat values (J/kg)

temperature. This process continues until the melting point or boiling point is reached, and then a change of state happens. If this is not done, the state will stay as it is. Some materials need more energy to raise their temperatures than others. It is important to realize that just as heat has to be **added** to increase temperature, it has to be **removed** if the temperature is to be reduced.

16.7 Specific heats

It is only fair to choose similar amounts and similar temperature rises if we are going to compare the energy needs of materials. The number of joules of energy required to raise the temperature of 1 kg of material 1 °C (1K) is known as the **specific heat capacity** (shc). Every material has a shc.

Water needs 4200 J of energy for every kilogram and every 1 °C temperature rise. Steam and ice are thought of as different materials, and they each have their own shc values.

16.8 Units of specific heat capacity

The units of shc are rather awkward. They are joules per kilogram per °C temperature rise (J/kg°C). Table 16.2 shows some shc values (column 4).

Material	Mass (kg)	Temp. rise (°C)	Energy needed for each kg°C (J/kg°C)	Total energy used (J)
Water	1	1	4200	4200
Water	2	1	4200	8400
Water	1	3	4200	12 600
Water	2	2	4200	16 800
Water	1	4	4200	16 800
Ice	1	1	2100	2100
Ice	1	2	2100	4200
Ice	4	1	2100	8400
Mercury	1	1	1400	1400
Iron	1	1	4500	4500
Gold	1	1	1300	1300

Table 16.2 Specific heat capacities

The energy shown in the last column of Table 16.2 is used to increase the vibrations of the molecules.

16.9 The mountaineer's meal

Now, it would be useful to see how a practical example works. (Latent heat **and** specific heat give you a lot to think about!)

Suppose a mountaineer needs to heat 2 kg of melting 'ice' to make his lunch. A sensible temperature for a hot drink is about 60 °C. How much energy will he have to use? (See Fig. 16.4.)

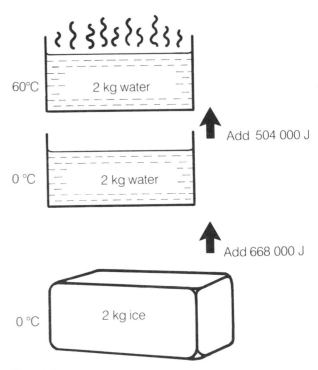

Fig. 16.4

These are the changes that have to take place:

(i) first the ice will need to be melted completely – **latent heat added**:

ENERGY USED = MASS × SPECIFIC LATENT HEAT
= 2 kg × 334 000 J/kg
= 668 000 J

(ii) then the water has to be heated up to 60 °C – **specific heat added**:

ENERGY USED = MASS × TEMPERATURE CHANGE
× SPECIFIC HEAT CAPACITY
= 2 kg × 60 °C × 4200 J/kg°C
= 504 000 J

There are two separate portions of energy to be added together to give the final energy total.
Total energy used is:
668 000 J + 504 000 J = 1 172 000 J

Activities

1 True steam is colourless. Fill a kettle with some water, switch it on and wait for it to boil. While it is boiling, look very carefully at the end of the spout. You should be able to see two separate regions where the steam emerges. In this area a change of state is taking place. Can you identify and explain the changes? Table 16.2 may help you to finish off these simple calculations:

Material	Mass (kg)	Temp. rise (°C)	Energy needed for each kg°C (J/kg°C)	Total energy used (J)
(a) Water	2	5	4200	?
(b) Water	10	1	4200	?
(c) Water	3	2	4200	?
(d) Water	6	1	4200	?

2 A very fortunate goldsmith found a 1 kg gold bar. He decided to melt it down and make some exciting jewelry (see Fig. 16.5). To start with he had to heat it up by 1000 °C to its melting point. How much heat energy must the goldsmith have supplied before he was able to pour the molten gold into the moulds he had prepared? (Use Table 16.2 and Table 16.1 to help you.)

Fig. 16.5

Make sure you have permission to try this next experiment.

3 You will need:
6 ice cubes
an old saucepan
a 0–100 °C thermometer
a watch
something to stir the ice cubes with

Put a cupful of water in the saucepan and add the ice cubes. Stir the mixture and measure the temperature (it should be very close to 0 °C). You are going to heat the mixture **very gently** over a cooking ring or flame (see Fig. 16.6).

Fig. 16.6

You should stir the mixture continuously and measure the temperature every minute until all the ice has melted and the temperature of the mixture reaches about 30 °C. Make a record of your readings. You should then plot them on a graph with axes like the ones in Fig. 16.3.

Brainteasers

4 Many vegetables suffer from 'frost damage'. What would be the purpose of keeping them in a cellar alongside a large tank of water during a bitterly cold winter's night? (*Hint*: look at Table 16.2.)

5 There is a pudding known as 'jam roly-poly'. It is made simply by rolling up jam in a layer of suet pudding. It is often served hot from the pan with the warning – 'Mind your tongue on the jam!' As they have both come from the same place, why is there no warning about the sponge?

Summary

Temperature is a measure of hotness, but heat is really a measure of the vibration of the molecules in a material. Latent, or hidden, heat energy is needed to change the state of a substance. During this change, the temperature remains constant.

Unit 17

Conduction (1)

17.1 Heat flow

Heat always travels from a hot place to a colder place. There are three ways in which heat energy can be passed around: **convection, radiation** and **conduction**. The last of these allows heat energy to travel through materials. Solids are best at conduction, because of the way in which their molecules are arranged.

Different materials conduct heat at different rates. They each have their own 'label' or value of thermal conductivity. Something that is good at allowing heat to travel through it has a high thermal conductivity, and something that is poor at letting heat travel through it has a low thermal conductivity.

A material with a very, very low conductivity would be called an **insulator**. These substances don't really allow much heat to travel through them at all. Generally, metals make good conductors, and non-metals, liquids and gases do not. Table 17.1 shows some good conductors and

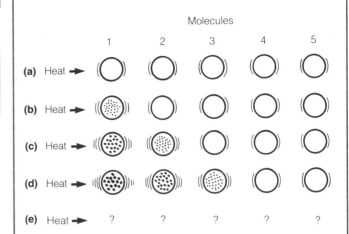

Fig. 17.1 What would be stage (e)?

some good insulators. They are in order and the most effective are at the top.

Conductors	Insulators
Silver	Air
Copper	Rubber
Gold	Paper
Aluminium	Teflon
Graphite	Wood
Brass	Water
Zinc	Brick
Tin	Glass
Cast Iron	Concrete
Mercury	Ice

Table 17.1 Which are the odd ones out? Why?

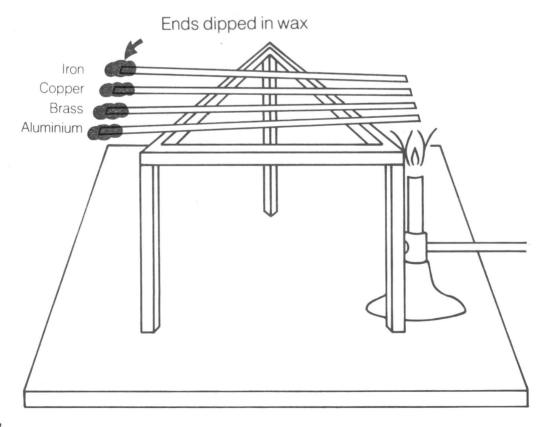

Ends dipped in wax

Iron
Copper
Brass
Aluminium

Fig. 17.2

17.2 Conduction and molecules

Solids tend to be the best conductors because of the way their molecules are arranged. They pass on heat energy in a similar way in which you play 'pass the parcel'. Fig. 17.1 shows the way in which heat energy is transferred.

Part (a) of the diagram has all the molecules vibrating gently. They would all be at the same temperature.

Part (b) introduces some heat energy. The first molecule in the line begins to vibrate more violently. It now has a higher temperature than the others.

Part (c) shows the conduction, or passing on, of some heat energy from the first molecule to the second. This, too, now begins to vibrate more violently.

Part (d) continues the conduction process. The temperature along the bar gradually increases as the heat energy travels from one end to the other.

17.3 Measuring conduction

There is a very simple method for measuring how well a material will conduct heat. The selection of materials to be compared are laid across the top of a tripod (see Fig. 17.2). A bunsen burner, with a roaring flame, is placed underneath. The far ends of the rods have been covered in candle wax. By watching and waiting for the wax to melt, it is easy to tell which is the better conductor.

We cannot really put a definite value or number to the conduction of heat by a material in this experiment. It would be more scientific to use the word 'compare' rather than 'measure'.

Activities

1 The conduction experiment from Section 17.3 is used to **compare** materials. You could make a **measure** of the conduction of a material by taking one simple measurement. What measurement would you make and how would you take it?

2 What is the purpose of the fins on the side of the motorcycle engine shown in Fig. 17.3?

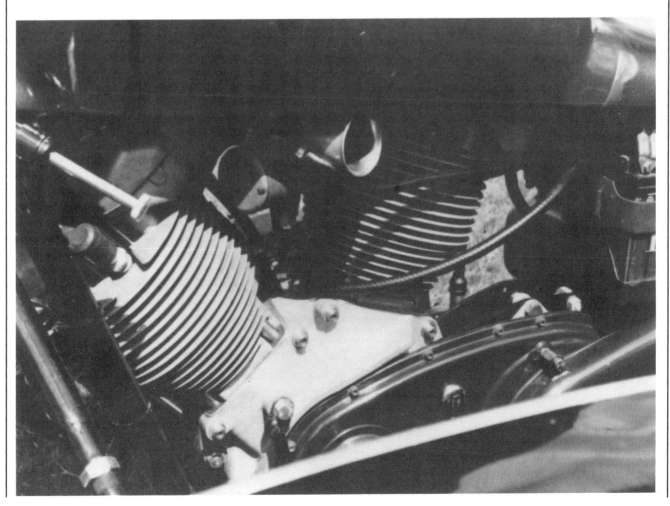

Fig. 17.3

Activities  continued

3 Many household items use conduction to their advantage. How many can you find? Some of them could be well hidden in places you might not expect.

4 In America they use 'sizzle sticks' with Bar-B-Qs. Kebabs are sometimes made with them. Another name for them is 'skewers'. What are they, what do they do and how do they work?

5 A cat's favourite place is often a pile of old newspapers or a carboard box? Why?

Make sure you have permission to do these next experiments. They are best performed over a sink or kitchen work surface.

Push the knitting needle right through the cork. This is now your handle. Make a small mark with a pen or pencil every 2.5 cm from the point of the needle. Light the candle and allow a drop of wax to drip on to the marks you have just made. Let them go cold.

Holding the needle by the handle place the point into the candle flame. Start timing. Time how long it takes for the first drop of wax to melt and then continue until the rest of the drops have melted. Is there any pattern or connection linking the time intervals?

Junior egg race

7 You are a contestant in an 'Egg Race'. The materials you receive are a box of bits and the card shown in Fig. 17.4.

JUNIOR EGG RACE

EGG RACE EQUIPMENT

A kettle full of very hot water
 (*HANDLE WITH CARE*)
An egg timer
1 steel ruler (30 cm)
1 long aluminium window handle
50 cm length copper piping
1 large plastic bowl
An all-metal knife (nickel)
A lead (graphite) pencil
A full butter dish
A can of orange juice

EGG RACE TASK

Produce by *MEASUREMENT* a list, containing 5 materials, with the best conductor at the top and the worst at the bottom.

Fig. 17.4 The 'Egg Race' card

6 You will need these bits and pieces for this simple experiment:
  a long metal knitting needle
  a candle
  a pen or pencil
  a watch
  a piece of cork

Summary

Heat energy can travel well through materials, especially solids/metals, by passing on vibrations from molecule to molecule. This method of heat flow is known as conduction.

Unit 18

Conduction (2)

18.1 Heat flow in fluids

As you will have done some work and experiments on conduction, you know that it depends on molecules being able to pass on the heat energy. The molecules can do this because they are in fixed positions and

The temperature is taken from the thermometer continuously. In this way it is possible to see if conduction takes place. Electrical energy is changed into heat by the heater coil. (The flow of electricity pushing itself through the wire creates friction inside the wire. Friction causes a heating effect, and so the coil warms up.) By conduction the coil passes on some heat to the water that is very close by. If the heater is left on for a very long time, there will probably be a considerable change in temperature, but this will not be due to conduction. Heat can travel in water, and you will find out more about this in the next Unit.

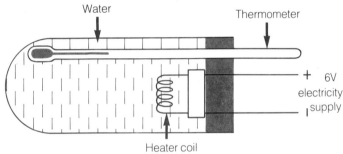

Fig. 18.1 Conduction in water

it is very easy to pass on the vibrations. The molecules in a fluid move. They will not be able to pass on vibrations to their next-door neighbours so easily. We have to find a way to keep the fluids still if we are to see if they are conductors or not.

18.2 Conduction by water (liquids)

The apparatus used in one experiment to investigate conduction in liquids is shown in Fig. 18.1.

18.3 Conduction by air (gases)

This is easy to demonstrate using the apparatus in Fig. 18.2. The equipment is very simple. Two thermometers are fitted in a cardboard tube. When the air at one end is hot the heater is removed and the covers are put on the ends of the tube. Nothing more is done to the apparatus, but the thermometers are watched for a while. The thermometer at the cold end rises only slowly if at all. Air is a bad conductor of heat.

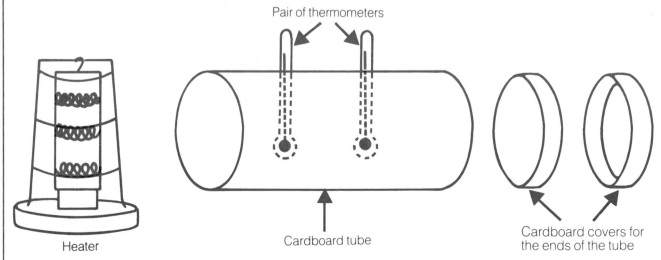

Fig. 18.2 Conduction in air

Unit 18 continued

18.4 Conduction at work

In the nineteenth century the enormous increase in coal output brought with it a large increase in fatal mine explosions. Methane, or firedamp, a gas found in coal mines is explosive when mixed with air and in contact with a naked flame. The miners used candles for illumination! In 1813 a society was formed to investigate ways of preventing these disasters. Sir Humphrey Davy was asked for advice and from this came the Davy Safety Lamp.

Fig. 18.3 shows the arrangement of a miner's safety lamp and way of demonstrating how it works. The flame is surrounded by a copper mesh. The air needed by the flame enters through this mesh. The heat from the flame is conducted away by the copper mesh. In this way any inflammable gases outside are not heated by the lamp flame, and so they do not ignite.

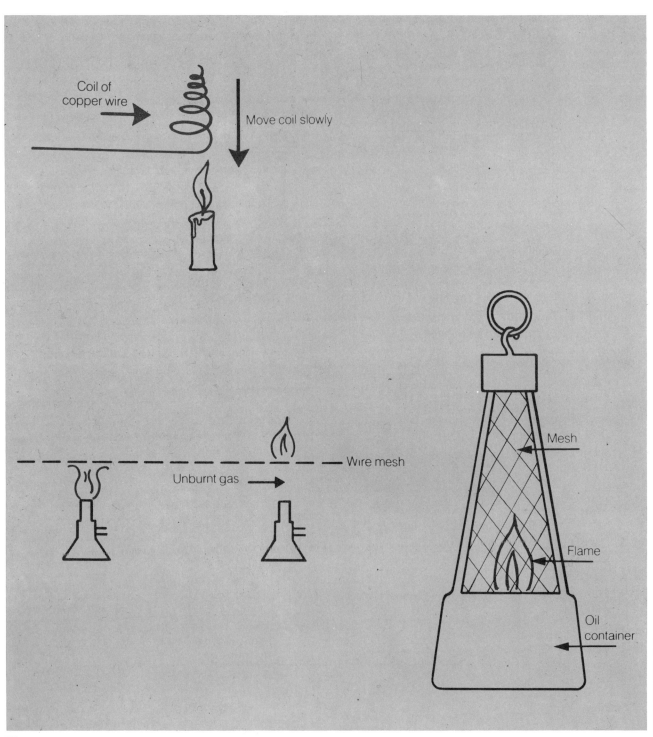

Fig. 18.3

Activities

1 For this experiment, you will need these pieces of equipment:

> two clean empty tin cans (with the paper labels removed)
> a saucepan
> a thermometer
> a watch
> some cotton wool
> some very hot water

Place one of the cans in the saucepan. Fill in the gap between the can and pan with the cotton wool. This provides a 'blanket' of still air around the can, and it is this you are testing for conduction. Very carefully fill both cans with the hot water. You are going to take the temperature of both cans every minute for 15 minutes (see Fig. 18.4).

Each time you take a measurement record it. You will then have two lists of temperatures. Make a up a table showing the temperatures and times. Draw the axes of temperature/time like the one in Fig. 16.3. On this, plot the temperatures for the can surrounded by cotton wool, for each minute. Then on the same axes plot the points obtained from the other can.

(a) How are the graphs different from one another?

(b) Do they **suggest** anything about the conduction of heat through air?

(c) This is an experiment about conduction. There are many simple ways the experiment can be improved. How many can you find?

(d) What practical use can you obtain from this experiment?

(e) Your graphs will probably end in mid-air. Keeping them as smooth as possible continue the graphs on until you run off the edge of the paper. This is a useful exercise to do, but can you think of the reason why?

> **These next experiments should be done with care and the permission of an adult. Ask them to check the apparatus you make up!**

2 Try making your own Davy Lamp. Wrap about 25 cm of thick copper wire around a pencil to form a coil. With some tweezers hold the coil above the flame of a candle (see Fig. 18.3). By experimenting, you should be able to make the coil extinguish the flame even though air is able to pass through it.

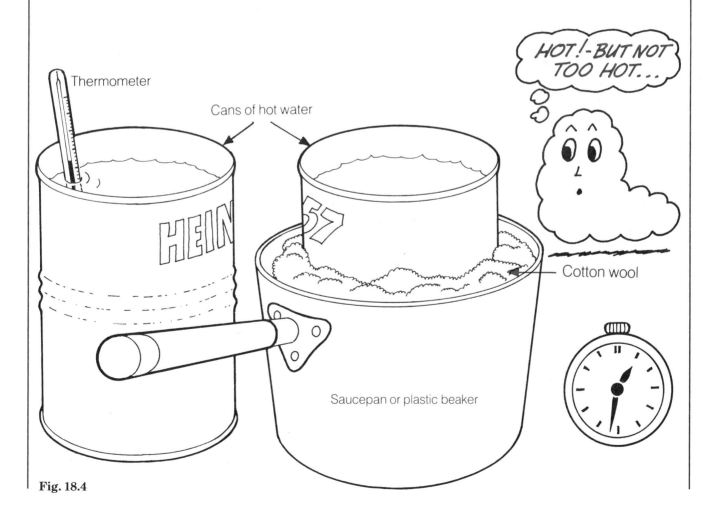

Fig. 18.4

Activities  continued

Brainteaser

3 Fig. 18.5 is a copy of the drawing and instructions that Andrew made during one of his science lessons. He had just started the experiment when the fire practice bell sounded. When he returned to the laboratory the ice had melted completely and there was no more. Using odds and ends that you might find lying around, devise a similar experiment to Andrew's and complete the observation section.

Summary

Conduction does not take place readily in liquids and gases. They are able to flow, and it should be easier for them to take heat with them rather than to pass it on from molecule to molecule.

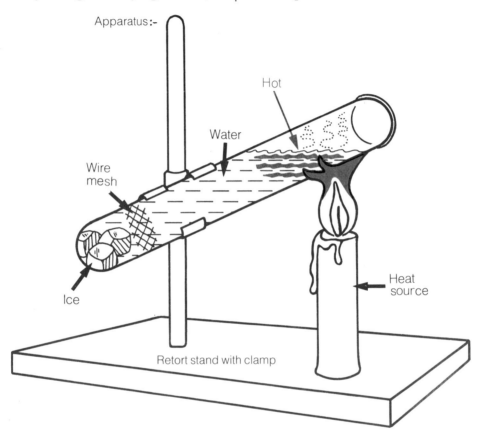

Apparatus:-

Hot

Water

Wire mesh

Ice

Retort stand with clamp

Heat source

METHOD:-

1. PART FILL TEST TUBE WITH WATER.

2. USE WIRE MESH TO MAKE ICE SINK.

3. KEEP TEST TUBE AT AN ANGLE.

4. GENTLY HEAT TOP PART OF TEST TUBE TILL THE WATER THERE STARTS TO BOIL.

5. WATCH FOR THE EFFECT OF THE HOT WATER AT THE TOP OF THE TEST TUBE ON THE ICE AT THE BOTTOM.

PRECAUTIONS:- ALWAYS KEEP TEST TUBE POINTED AWAY FROM PEOPLE.

OBSERVATIONS:-

Fig. 18.5 Conduction of heat in water

Unit 19

Convection currents (1)

19.1 Moving molecules

One of the ways in which heat energy can be transferred is from molecule to molecule. In fluids, however, the molecules themselves move. If they are given extra energy before they move off to somewhere else then they will take that energy with them. The process of molecules travelling with extra energy is called **convection**. It is a little similar to a rugby player (the molecule) running with the ball (some energy). This method of heat flow cannot work with solids.

Fig. 19.1 Convection currents

19.2 Taking up space

If a molecule is vibrating more violently because it has more energy, then it will have to take up more room. This is important because it means that you will get fewer molecules in a particular space.

Fig. 19.1 shows two identical boxes filled with molecules. Box (a) is filled with very energetic molecules. There is room for more molecules with less energy in box (b). The molecules in box (a) will appear to be 'lighter' than the molecules in box (b) (because they have more energy). In a mixture, the more energetic ones will rise leaving the less energetic ones below. Molecules are now on the move. A convection current has started!

19.3 Convection currents in water

Water is a fairly good insulator, but it will transfer heat well by convection. Most homes now have 'running' hot and cold water. Convection currents play an important part in many household water systems. Fig. 19.2 (on the next page) shows a typical domestic hot water piping system. This example contains a boiler to heat the water, a hot water storage tank that also has in it an electric immersion heater and a cold water supply tank.

Table 19.1 shows some of the special design features of the system.

Feature	Reason
Expansion pipe	Allows air bubbles and steam to escape
Cold water must enter the hot water storage tank at the bottom	Cold water will stay at the bottom of the tank and not mix with the hot water
The hot water pipe must be at the top of the tank	Hot water will rise and so will be drawn off first
The immersion heater is small and at the top of the tank	This allows the heating of a small amount of water quickly if needed

Table 19.1 Special design features of the hot water system shown in Fig. 19.2

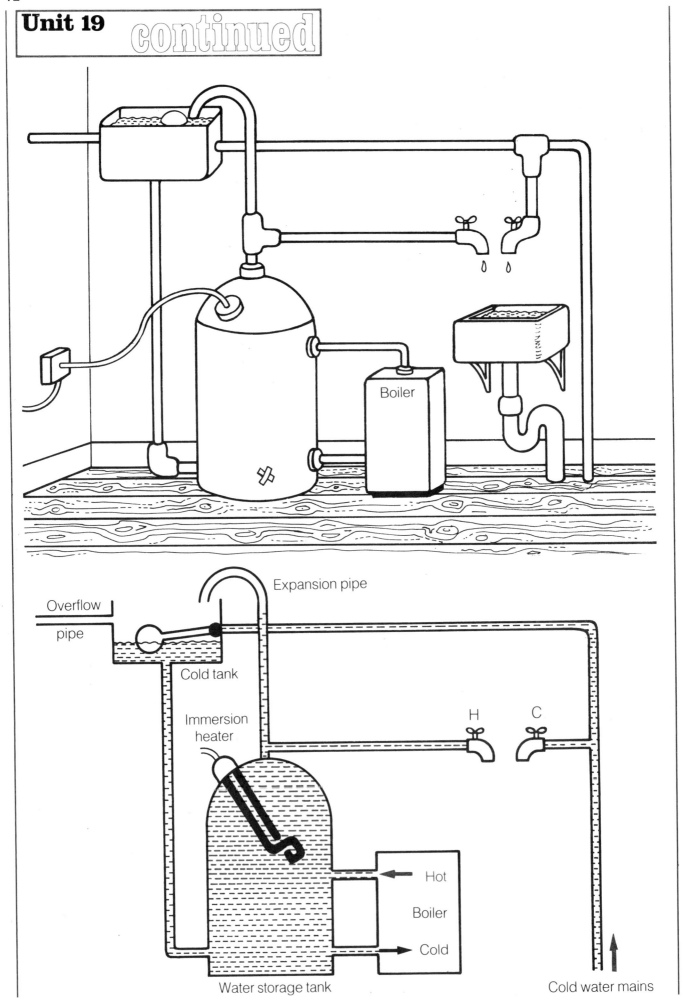

Expansion pipe

Overflow
pipe

Cold tank

Immersion
heater

H   C

Hot

Boiler

Cold

Water storage tank

Cold water mains

Fig. 19.2 Hot water system

Activities

1 You will need the following bits and pieces for this experiment:

    an empty jar or clear glass/plastic tumbler
    some hot water
    a large ice cube
    a tube of Smarties

Fill the jar or glass with hot water. (Care is needed here, because the glass may crack if the water is too hot.) Wait a few moments, until the water has stopped swirling around and is fairly still. Choose two or three of the darker coloured Smarties and carefully drop them into the water. Watch closely as you slowly and gently drop the ice cube into the water.

(a) What do you notice about the water next to the ice cube?

(b) Has anything happened to the Smarties?

(c) How do the Smarties help you observe convection currents?

(d) What does this experiment tell you about hot and cold water?

2 Look at Fig. 19.2.

(a) Why is the level of the water in the expansion pipe higher than the level of the water in the cold water tank?

(b) When the immersion heater is being used, why will water below the heater not be heated by convection currents?

3 Draw out the diagrams in Fig. 19.3, and then mark on them where you would place a source of heat that will cause the convection currents shown.

4 Many car engines are water cooled. The cooling process involves convection. Find out more details of how water flows around an engine and how cooling takes place.

5 Electric kettles have an immersion heater in them (the element). These are placed near the base of the kettle. Why are they put there, and what methods are used to transfer heat energy to the water?

6 From a roll of aluminium cooking foil, cut a strip about 1 cm wide and 10 cm long. Now cut up this strip into **very small** pieces. Half-fill a saucepan with water and sprinkle the foil pieces onto the water. Make sure the foil sinks. Place the saucepan on a cooker ring and begin to heat it gently. Watch carefully what happens to the foil as the water warms up.

(a) From this experiment what evidence is there for the existence of convection currents in water?

(b) When you first sprinkled the foil on the water, it should have reminded you of some physics in an earlier Unit. What is it?

(c) There may be another observation you can make about the foil as the water heated – but what?

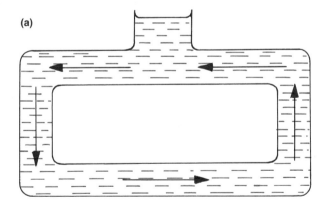

(a)

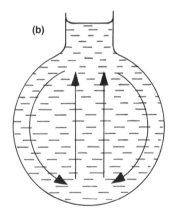

(b)

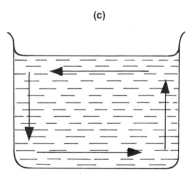

(c)

Fig. 19.3

74

Activities continued

Brainteasers

7 For this experiment you will need two jam jars
(which must have the same sized necks!), a piece
of fairly stiff card, some ink or food colouring
(N.B. **food colouring can stain badly!**) and
some hot and cold water. This experiment is best
done over a sink.

Fill one of the jam jars to the brim with cold
water. Fill the second jar to the brim with very
warm water and add two or three drops of the
colouring. Allow this to mix thoroughly. Place the
card over the neck of the jar filled with cold water.
Place your hand on the card and turn the jar
upside down. Very carefully place the jar/card
(exactly) on top of the warm water jar (see
Fig. 19.4). Try not to spill water from either jar.

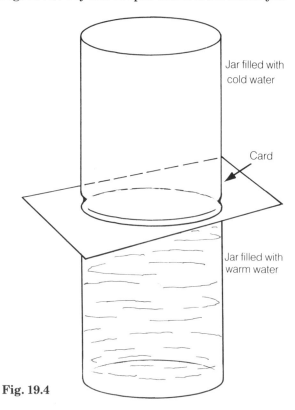

Fig. 19.4

Very carefully, and as quickly as you can, pull out
the card from between the jars. You should be
able to see various things happening. What do
you notice? How many observations can you
make? Write them out in a list.

What would be the effect if a second colour
were added to the cold water jar?

Fig. 19.5 shows a modification to the piece of
card. It has had two holes made in it. One hole is
quite small. It is about the size of a pencil point.
The second hole is much larger and is big enough
to have the clear outer tube of a biro pushed
through it. The card is not to be removed for this
experiment.

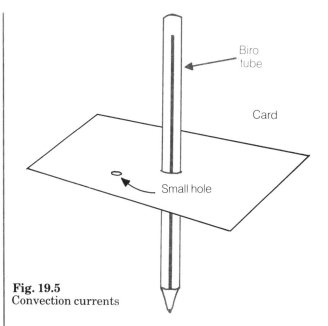

Fig. 19.5
Convection currents

Repeat the experiment. You will have to be very
quick at putting the jars on top of each other this
time. Write out a second list of your observations
and compare them with the first. Are there any
changes?

Fig. 19.6

8 Andrew and Anne had just been for a very
quick dip while Edward looked after their
belongings. Andrew came out of the sea
complaining that the water was cold. Anne told
him that he was talking rubbish and that the
water was quite warm. Edward, who had been
sitting on the beach listening, went in for a swim
to settle the argument and came back saying they
were both right. Can you suggest a reason for
Edward saying what he did?

Summary

Convection currents take place because molecules
move. As they do so they take heat energy with
them.

Unit 20

Convection currents (2)

20.1 Convection currents in air

It is very simple to demonstrate these air currents. Fig. 20.1 shows this. A smoke trail may be made very effectively using a piece of smouldering string.

As the hot air rises above the candle, so more air replaces it from underneath. This enters the box from the other chimney and so brings the smoke with it. This particular example of convection is of considerable practical use. In the days before air pumps, the method was used to provide a continuous supply of fresh air to the mineworkers underground, although having fire underground presented problems of its own!

On a much larger scale, convection currents are going on all around us. They are responsible for much of the weather, particularly the wind system and cloud formation (see Fig. 20.2).

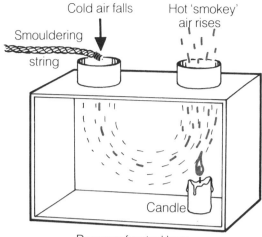

Fig. 20.1 Convection currents in air

Fig. 20.2

Unit 20 continued

Sea breezes (Fig. 20.2) are convection currents. During the day the land heats up much more quickly than the sea. The air above the land warms quickly and rises. This is replaced by cooler air blowing in from the sea. The result is an on-shore breeze going from sea to land. During the night the land cools much more quickly than the sea and its temperature drops faster. This time warm air rises from above the water to be replaced by cooler air from above the land. The result is an off-shore breeze going from the land to the sea.

(Land hot)　(Sea warm)

(Land cold)　(Sea warm)

Fig. 20.2

Draughts can cause considerable nuisance, and much is done to reduce them. Unwanted they may be, but they do perform a useful task as they provide much-needed ventilation in a room (see Fig. 20.3). A room with a coal or gas fire would soon become very uncomfortable and stuffy if the air were not continually being changed.

The Romans used charcoal fires to provide convection currents for underfloor central heating (see Fig. 20.3).

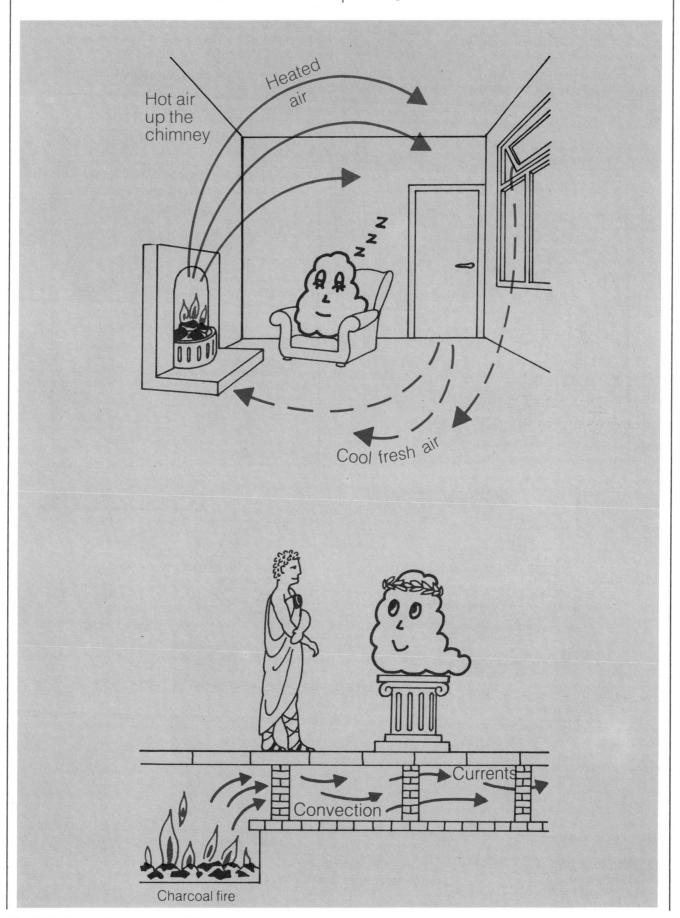

Fig. 20.3 Convection currents and heating

Activities

1 The experiment described in Fig. 20.1 can be done very easily at home. All you need is:

a small piece of candle
some aluminium cooking foil
a piece of string
some matches
an empty jam jar

Can you find a way to do it?

2 Fig. 20.4 shows two convection models to make. You will need:

some paper
a pair of scissors
some crayons
a candle

Make up a model and test it. Can you now find a (very) practical use for the fan or the snake on its own?

3 **Ask permission before you start this experiment.** Fig. 20.3 shows how convection currents can move air around a room. As the

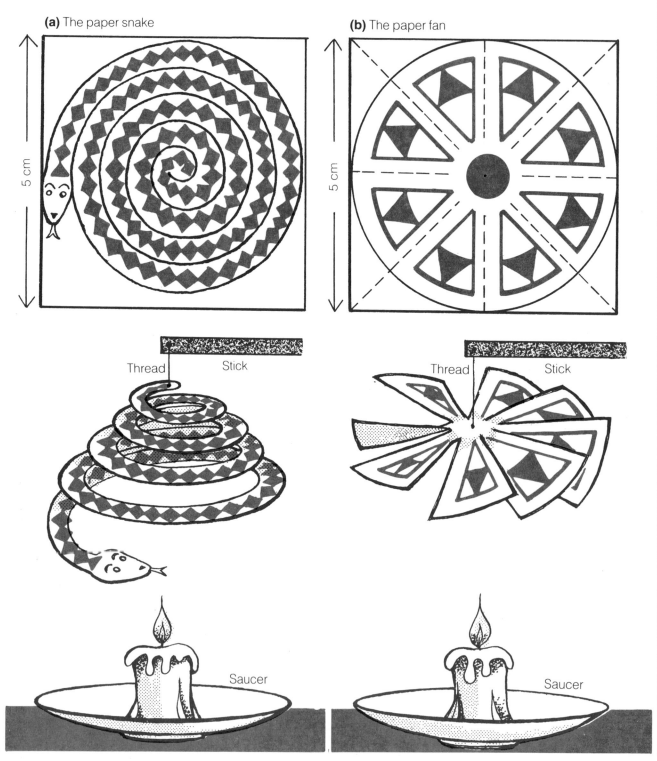

(a) The paper snake

(b) The paper fan

Fig. 20.4 Convection models

warm air rises cool air moves in to take its place. This experiment will let you follow the convection currents around the rooms in your home. Fig. 20.5 is a see-through view into a house. Make a similar sketch using your house as the model. **With great care** light one end of a long piece of string (about 1 metre in length). Blow out the flame to leave the string smouldering. The string will leave a smoke trail wherever it goes. You can use this smoke trail to track down any currents of air. On your drawing you can plot the directions of these currents. **When you have finished with the string extinguish it in water.**

4 The photograph in Fig. 20.6 shows Concorde about to take off. What does this particular picture of Concorde have to do with 'convection currents'?

Brainteaser

5 The reason's the same:

(a) Flames can lift you into the sky.
(b) It's better to crawl out of a smoke-filled room.
(c) A kilt keeps a Scotsman's knees warm.
(d) The freezer compartment of a fridge is always at the top.

Brainbuster

6 Philip and his sister Liz had spent the day by the sea. It was now early evening and time to go. They walked along the beach to the car-park:
    'Funny' said Philip 'It's been windy all day and now it's time to go the wind has stopped.'

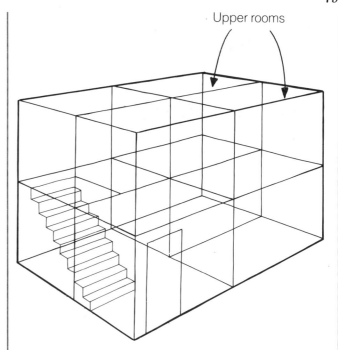

Fig. 20.5

'I was just thinking the same thing' said Liz, 'It's not our lucky day!'.
Luck probably had nothing to do with it. Why not?

Summary

Fluid materials that do not conduct heat can be made to transfer heat energy by convection.

Fig. 20.6

Unit 21

Radiation

21.1 Death rays

In about 214 BC the Romans attacked the town of Syracuse. The Greek scientist Archimedes is supposed to have saved the town by burning the Roman fleet. This is thought to have been done with many mirrors on shore directing the sun's rays on each ship in turn and causing them to burst into flames.

Archimedes used the sun's **rays**. They could just as easily have been called **waves** or **radiations**.

21.2 Thermal energy

We have already met (Units 17 to 20) two methods of heat transfer – conduction and convection. The third method of heat transfer is known as **thermal radiation**, or 'radiation' for short. These radiations or waves are close relatives of red light. They are sometimes called **infrared**.

When these energy waves fall on an object some of them may be taken in, or absorbed. As everything is made of molecules, then it must be the molecules that absorb the energy. When molecules absorb energy they vibrate more – they begin to heat up and their temperature increases.

Fig. 21.1 (a) An airport at night: thermal image

21.3 Giving away energy

All objects emit infrared/thermal radiation — even you! If you sit in front of a fire on a cold evening you feel warm and comfortable. You do not keep on getting hotter and hotter. As well as absorbing heat from the fire you also give heat away. You **radiate**, or emit, heat too! The hotter an object is the more energy it will give away. Special cameras can be used to take pictures of objects emitting thermal radiation, and the pictures they take show much more than normal photographs (see Fig. 21.1).

21.4 Infrared rays

As these rays belong to the same family as light they share some things in common, although they cannot be seen by the human eye. They can be used with mirrors and lenses. Most importantly, they travel at the same speed and they do not need a material to travel in. They can travel in the vacuum of space. This sets radiation apart from convection and conduction, which both need a material if they are going to transfer heat energy. The sun is the largest radiator we have nearby.

Fig. 21.1 (b) An airport at night: normal image

Unit 21 continued

21.5 Absorbers and radiators

Some surfaces are better than others at absorbing thermal radiaton. White is a very popular colour in hot countries (Fig. 21.2), because it reduces the amount of radiation absorbed.

Good absorbers are good radiators
(The best absorbers are dull and dark)
Poor radiators are poor absorbers
(The worst absorbers are bright and shiny)

If a material is poor at absorbing heat energy, then it must be reflecting it away again:

Poor absorbers are good reflectors

The Victorians used the idea of radiation to great advantage when they made cast iron fireplaces (Fig. 21.3). They had a large metal surround that was usually painted black.

Fig. 21.3 Why so large and why so dark?

Fig. 21.2 Why is white such a popular colour?

Activities

1 Why are most fridges and freezers white? There is something very different about the back of a fridge? What is the purpose of this difference?

2 This experiment needs to be done on a reasonably warm, sunny day. You will need a thermometer and the cooperation of some car owners! Ask them if you can take the temperature of the inside of their cars. (The cars should all have been in the sun for a little while with the doors and windows shut.) Record the temperature of each car and its colour. When you have collected several results, rearrange them to show which colour is best/worst at absorbing heat.

3 Gardeners sometimes add soot to the soil. Apart from any goodness this may or may not give to the plants is there any other reason for doing it?

4 Baked jacket potatoes can be very tasty. One method of cooking them is to wrap them in foil before putting them in the oven or on the open fire. Kitchen foil has one shiny surface and one dull surface. Does it matter which finish is on the outside of something to be cooked? Can you devize an experiment to test this?

5 For this experiment, you will need:
    aluminium foil
    a candle
    a black felt-tipped marker pen

Cut out two 4 cm × 4 cm squares of foil. Use the marker pen on one of the squares to make one surface completely black. Wet the back of one hand and stick the foil, dark side up, onto the wet patch of your hand. Wet your other hand in the same way and stick onto it the other piece of foil, shiny side up. Light the candle. Start with your hands about 10 cm away from the candle with the pieces of foil facing the flame (see Fig. 21.4). Can your hands tell which surface is better at absorbing heat?

6 Central heating radiators are rather badly named. Why is this, and what would need to be done to make them live up to their name?

7 Look around your home for examples of 'radiators'. Some are designed to radiate heat energy and some are not. Make a list like this:

Things designed to radiate	Things designed not to radiate

8 You can buy 35 mm infrared film! If you try some, be sure to read the film instructions very carefully. Take some pictures, and get them developed. You might be in for a surprise when you see the photographs.

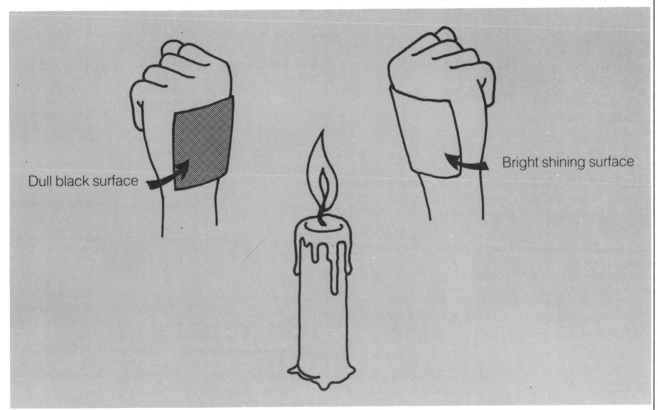

Dull black surface

Bright shining surface

Fig. 21.4 Good or bad absorbers?

84

9 For this experiment you will need:
a small balloon
an empty washing-up liquid bottle
some black paint
Blow up the balloon once and let it down. This takes the 'newness' out of the rubber. Put the balloon over the neck of the bottle and place it in the sun. Leave it for a little while and see what happens. Try again but this time when the bottle has been painted black. Are there any differences this time?

With the help of a tape-measure, could you use this apparatus for anything else?

Fig. 21.5 Black is best?

10 The apparatus shown in Fig. 21.6 is a Crooke's Radiometer. They are quite often seen in school laboratories and can sometimes be bought as 'curious toys'. Four vanes, rather like paddle-wheels, are pivoted on top of a pointer. It is free to rotate. Energy in the form of radiation (infrared and light) enters the glass bulb and strikes the vanes.

(a) Which side of the vanes (polished or black), will absorb the energy and which side will reflect the energy?

(b) Which side of the vanes will heat up the most?

(c) What will happen to the air molecules nearest the sides with most energy?

(d) In which direction will the vanes rotate?

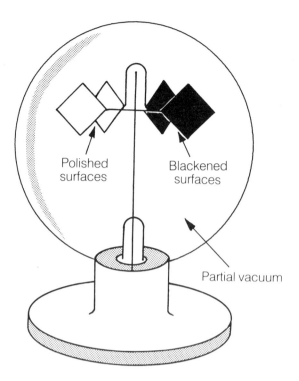

Fig. 21.6 Crooke's radiometer – in which direction will it rotate?

Brainteasers

11 What is the link between infrared radiation, heat energy and kinetic energy? How would you use all three to describe the way an object cools down?

12 Heat radiation reaches us from the sun. It travels at approximately 300 000 km/s for 148 000 000 km. How old (in minutes and seconds) is the heat energy when it arrives here? Use this equation:

$$\frac{\text{Distance}}{\text{Speed}} = \text{Time}$$

Summary

Heat waves – rays – radiations are the same thing – energy. An alternative name is infrared radiation. Unlike convection and conduction, it needs no material or medium to travel in.

Unit 22

Insulators

22.1 Staying alive

Animals must have heat to live. Body heat is made from the everyday fuels that are eaten and the oxygen that is breathed in. Perhaps you have heard of people and animals who have died of exposure – lack of clothing and shelter. People speak quite wrongly about 'keeping out the cold'. They really mean **keeping in the heat**. Heat only travels one way, and that's from hot to cold. It is important to conserve energy of every type, and not just because it is becoming more expensive and less abundant. Heat will escape at the first opportunity. The greater the temperature difference between an object and its surroundings the quicker the heat loss.

22.2 The Thermos flask

This is designed to reduce the transfer of heat (Fig. 22.1). It has to be a barrier to convection, conduction and radiation. The insulation works against heat flow in both directions, and so it keeps hot things hot and cold things cold.

Convection: the vacuum between the glass walls prevents convection currents completely.

Conduction: this is also completely prevented by the vacuum.

Radiation: The infrared radiation is more difficult to stop because it is the one method of heat flow that can travel through a vacuum. This is greatly reduced by the two brightly silvered surfaces of the glass, which bounce the radiation back into the flask.

The stopper is made of cork or other similar good insulating material.

22.3 Clouds

These play an important part in insulating the Earth! They reflect some of the infrared radiation given off from the ground. Without clouds, very hot days can lead to very cold nights and even frost!

At certain times of the year some crops and plants are more likely to suffer damage from low temperatures. Fruit growers make artificial clouds in their orchards to protect their crops when they think it is going to be a cold night.

Fig. 22.1 The Thermos flask

Unit 22 continued

22.4 Frozen fish fingers

Water is an insulator, and so is ice. Ice floats on water. (That is very strange by itself because ice is a solid and it floats on its own liquid!) During the winter many lakes and ponds freeze over (Fig. 22.2). Once ice has formed, it acts as an insulating layer for the remaining water. This helps to reduce further heat loss. The results would be catastrophic for marine life if this were not so.

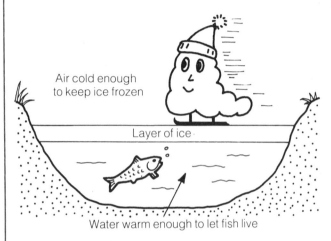

Air cold enough to keep ice frozen

Layer of ice

Water warm enough to let fish live

Fig. 22.2 Insulating properties of ice

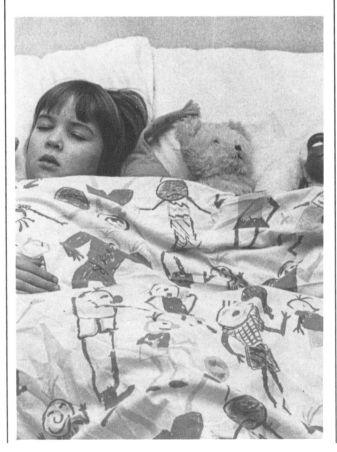

Fig. 22.3

22.5 Continental quilts

When we go to sleep many of our bodily functions go into low gear. Heat production is usually associated with activity so this reduces when we are asleep. Sleep is a necessity and we cannot go without it.

Unless you live in a very warm climate all the year round, an artificial method of heat control will be needed during cold spells. Some sort of 'blanket' or insulated covering is usual (Fig. 22.3).

Blankets keep you warm because they trap pockets of insulating air. They are made from closely woven materials and this can make them quite heavy. Continental quilts (duvets) do the same job in keeping you warm. As they are made from feathers or an artificial material that can be fluffed up they are much lighter than blankets. They originated in northern Scandinavia where the winters are very cold. Since they have been introduced into this country they have become very popular. Apart from being lighter they have the advantage that they can be shaken up (trapping more air pockets) when the weather is cold and flattened (trapping less air) when the weather is warmer.

The insulating properties are rated with a **tog value** (see Fig. 22.4). The higher the tog value the warmer the quilt.

Fig. 22.4

Activities

1 When used properly, under a shirt for example, a string vest is very effective as an insulator. How do a lot of holes keep you warm? Would the vest be as effective if it were used on its own?

2 Walk bare footed on some carpet and then on a tiled or stone floor. What do you notice? Can you explain your observation?

3 Double glazing is an effective insulator. Some have a vacuum in the gap between the panes of glass and others have it filled with air. What is the difference in insulating properties between the two methods? Each method has one possible disadvantage. Can you find out what it is?

4 During the colder winter months, birds sometimes seem much fatter. This has nothing to do with what they have just eaten. What is the cause of this?

5 What equipment would you need to investigate which was the best insulating material from the following:

    feathers
    fur
    cotton wool
    felt

Could you devise an experiment to do this?

You may need to use a library to help you with these next few questions.

6 Why do Eskimos live in ice houses? Many of their clothes are made from animal furs. There is a right and wrong way to make such clothes for use in arctic conditions. How would you make them? What else can you discover about how they survive in such low temperatures? (Canoeists learn a technique called the Eskimo roll. Can you find out what it is, and why it is important?)

7 The space shuttle is covered in insulating tiles (Fig. 22.5(a)). Space suits and other space craft (Fig. 22.5 (b)) do not use these tiles. How do they provide themselves with insulation? What range of temperatures do they have to cope with?

Fig. 22.5 (a)

Activities continued

Fig. 22.5 (b)

8 What can you find out about tog values? Collect some leaflets about some of the various continental quilts available and compare them. What are the different types of insulating material found in a duvet?

9 Some years ago eiderdowns were popular as bed coverings though they are not so fashionable now. They are named after their filling material. You sometimes see notices in the windows of dry cleaners' shops offering a service which converts an eiderdown into a duvet. What can you find out about 'eiderdown'?

10 The photograph in Fig. 22.6 shows an unfortunate character living rough. During cold weather an important job of the day is to look for some sort of bedding to keep warm at night. Why are materials such as cardboard boxes much sought after?

11 PHYSICS IN HISTORY Read this then answer the questions that follow.

The Dewar Flask

The vacuum theory is well understood. It had been used by an Italian, Evangelista Torricelli, in 1643 when he invented the mercury barometer. Sir James Dewar was having a problem keeping things cold. He was making large quantities of liquid oxygen and liquid hydrogen, but they were boiling away almost immediately. He used his knowledge of conduction, convection and radiation to invent the vacuum flask in 1892. This came to be known as the Dewar Flask. He made one for his young son in 1902, but his mother-in-law wondered how effective it would be and made a 'woolly cosy' (Fig. 22.7) for it!

Fig. 22.6   89

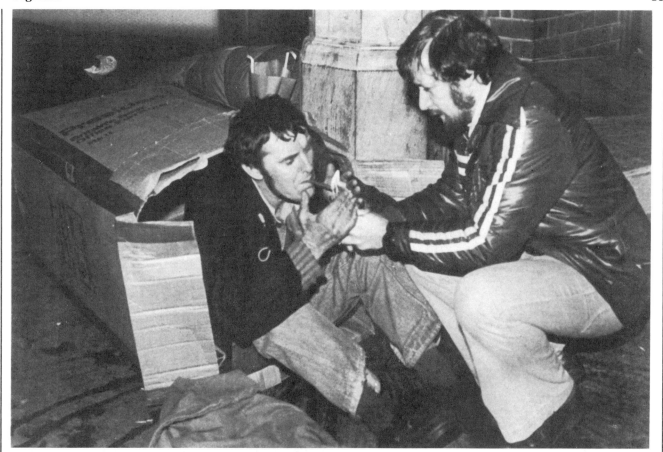

Fig. 22.7 Mother-in-law's cosy!

A competition to name this new convenience was set up by Reinhold Burger in 1904. This resulted in the new name – Thermos Flask. These flasks went to the Antarctic with Shackleton and to Everest with Hilary.

(a) How did the vacuum flask come to be invented?

(b) Find out the boiling points of liquid oxygen and liquid hydrogen.

(c) Why did James Dewar's mother-in-law waste her time making a cosy for the flask?

(d) For what reasons are these flasks useful on expeditions?

(e) Why is 'thermos' a sensible name for this invention?

Brainteaser

12 In addition to its insulating properties, in what other way can the ice layer help prevent heat loss from the pond?

Summary

Insulators and insulating materials are becoming more important as energy conservation becomes more important. Nature provides many examples of effective insulation.

Unit 23

Heating houses

23.1 Energy loss

In the United Kingdom the winters are cold with snow and ice, but the summers are warm. Different parts of the world have to cope with different types of climate. Australia is a very warm country all year round. The problem there is to keep buildings cool all the time.

We have to keep our homes warm in winter and cool in summer, so we need to have well-insulated houses. In this way we hope that they will stay at the temperature we want, regardless of local weather conditions. Fig. 23.1 shows the typical heat loss from a house without improved insulation.

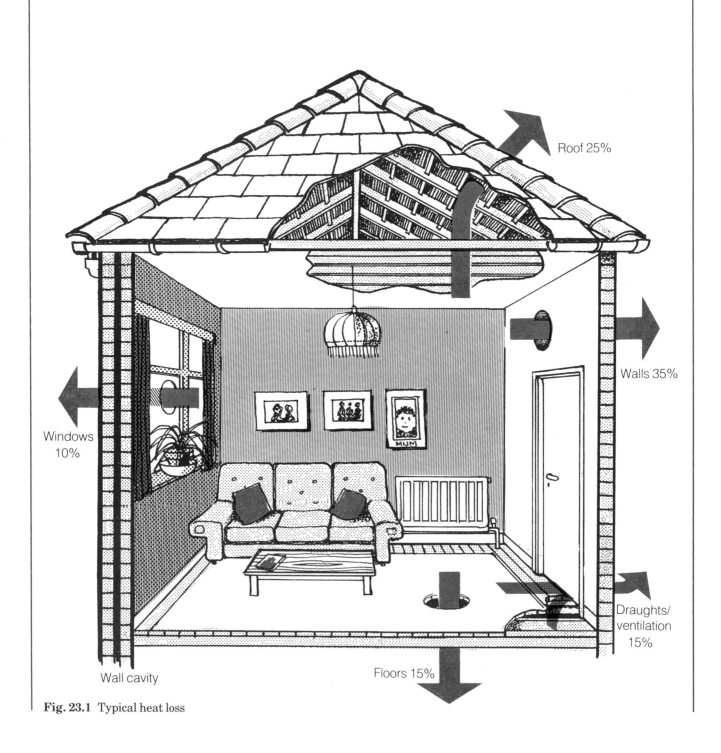

Roof 25%

Walls 35%

Windows 10%

Draughts/ ventilation 15%

Wall cavity

Floors 15%

Fig. 23.1 Typical heat loss

23.2 Energy savers

Energy loser	Remedy	Energy loss reduced
Walls	Fill the outer cavity walls with plastic foam or mineral fibre	From 35% to 15%
Roof	Mineral or glass fibre insulation in the loft	From 25% to 5%
Windows	Replace windows with double glazing	From 10% to 5%
Floors	Thick carpets and tiles	From 15% to 10%
Draughts	Most draughts can be stopped with draught excluders, although fresh air is needed for health	?

Table 23.1 Energy savers

The energy savers in Table 23.1 have reduced heat loss by half, or 50%. The saving from draught excluders would still have to be added to give a final energy saving.

Some specially designed houses (Fig. 23.2) have computer-controlled devices to save energy.

23.3 Automatic control

Time switches are used to programme part of the household heating system. In this way the heating is used as required and not left on permanently. Individual rooms can be heated at certain times and not others.

Thermostats are devices that control the temperature values of rooms or appliances. A room may have its heating system continuously turned on and off by a thermostat. This maintains a constant temperature and so saves fuel.

Outside controllers are used to switch on the heating system in a house when the outside temperature drops below a minimum value. This is particularly useful in avoiding frozen pipes and keeping a steady temperature in a house that is unoccupied.

The house shown in Fig. 23.2 is an example of the use of modern technology to control energy needs. The idea of energy control is not only to try and reduce heating bills but to help conserve precious energy resources.

Fig. 23.2 House with computer-controlled energy-saving devices

Activities

1 Copy out Table 23.2. Leave some extra blank spaces for any other energy wasters. Work your way around your own home and check on the various methods of insulation that have been installed. Fill out the Home Energy Survey. You may find when you have completed it that it is possible to save quite a lot of energy. It is only worthwhile making changes if the energy costs saved are more than the insulation costs. Double glazing may reduce heat loss by 5%, but it may take 10 years for the energy savings to pay for having it put in. What energy savers can you suggest from your survey that would save money as well as energy?

2 There are other ways of 'double glazing' windows without using the specially made window units. Can you make any suggestions for do-it-yourself, inexpensive double glazing?

3 Make a collection of leaflets about double glazing. Find out what triple glazing is.

4 The photograph in Fig. 23.3 shows a row of terraced houses. It was taken the day after quite a heavy snowfall. Can you tell which of the houses might belong to the author of a Physics text book?

Two houses in the row look somewhat out of place. They have had 'stone-cladding' added to their front walls. Apart from a change in appearance could these alterations have any other effect on the houses?

5 What are Kitemarks and what can you find out about the one shown in Fig. 23.4?

Table 23.2

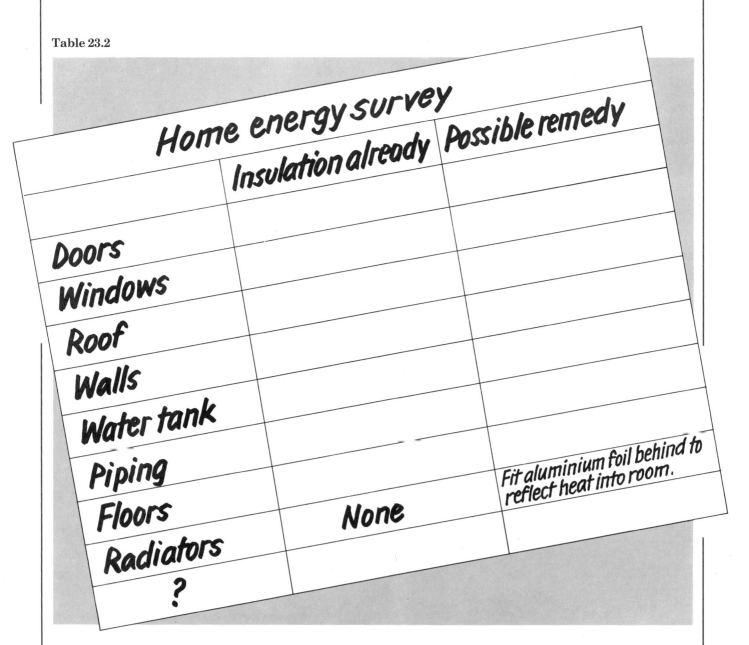

Home energy survey	Insulation already	Possible remedy
Doors		
Windows		
Roof		
Walls		
Water tank		
Piping		
Floors	None	Fit aluminium foil behind to reflect heat into room.
Radiators		
?		

Fig. 23.3

Fig. 23.4 The Kitemark

Activities continued

6 The diagram in Fig. 23.5 is typical of many loft insulation materials. It gives information about:

(a) the material used

(b) the thickness

(c) a value for thermal conductivity of 0.04 (this indicates how well it conducts heat)

(d) R-value of 2.5

Find as many different alternatives to this example of insulation as you can. Compare the information you find with the information here. Do the different makes of insulation share anything in common? What does the 'R-value' stand for?

7 You will probably know of several different ways of providing heat in the home, e.g. open fires or central heating. Find a working example of each heater listed in Table 23.3. They each give out heat by convection, conduction or radiation (or a mixture of the three). Copy out and complete Table 23.3.

Heater	Main method of heating
(a) Open fire	
(b) Electric bar fire	
(c) Radiator (made of copper and lightly painted)	
(d) Convector heater	
(e) Gas fire	

Table 23.3 Heater table

Brainteaser

8 A typical air gap between the two panes of glass of a double glazed window is 20 mm. Why is this distance important, and what could happen if the distance were smaller or larger?

Summary

Valuable heat energy is all too easily lost from buildings. This can usually be reduced by simple, inexpensive methods of insulation.

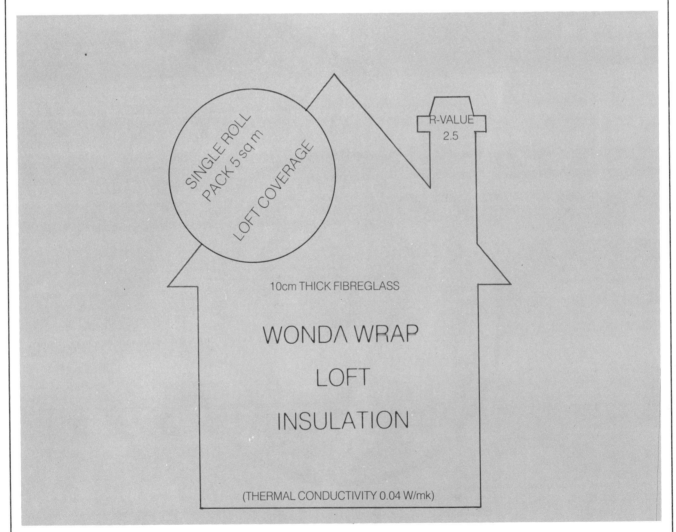

SINGLE ROLL PACK 5 sq m LOFT COVERAGE

R-VALUE 2.5

10cm THICK FIBREGLASS

WONDA WRAP LOFT INSULATION

(THERMAL CONDUCTIVITY 0.04 W/mk)

Fig. 23.5 How many different varieties can you find?

Unit 24

Cells

24.1 Cells and batteries

A **cell** just changes one kind of energy into another. It is a single unit capable of producing electricity. If two or more cells are connected together so that they push electricity in the same direction then this is known as a **battery** of cells. Batteries are usually labelled in **volts** (V), e.g., 3 V, 6 V.

A cell makes up part of an electric circuit. It has two **terminal connections** (known as **electrodes**) labelled **positive** (+) and **negative** (−). The positive electrode is called the **anode** (+) and the negative electrode is called the **cathode** (−).

24.2 Cells and symbols

Fig. 24.1 shows the circuit symbols for cells and batteries in various arrangements.

24.3 Cells and circuits

When cells are put in circuits, it is important that they are connected the right way round. If two cells are connected in opposite directions, they will be trying to send electricity in opposite directions. They will be 'pushing' against each other. If they are equal in 'strength', then no electricity will flow at all.

Whenever an electricity supply forms part of a circuit, it is **always** good practice to have another component, such as a bulb, in the circuit too. If this is not done, and a **short-circuit** (a direct connection between the two terminals) is made, then the electrical energy will be wasted in a very short time. (With much larger values of electrical energy this can be very dangerous.) Activity 3 should show this very clearly!

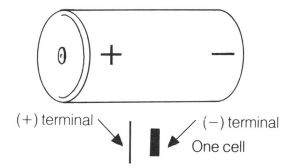

(+) terminal   (−) terminal
One cell

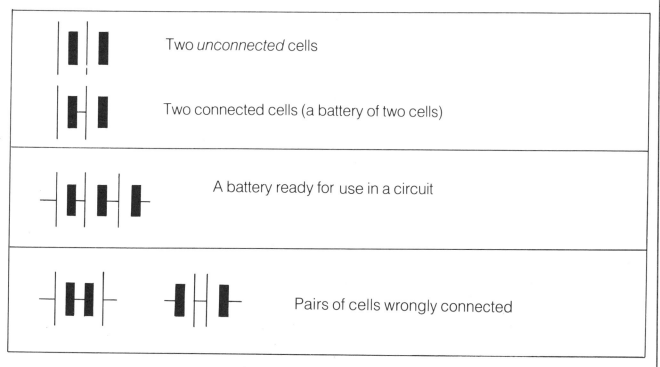

Two *unconnected* cells

Two connected cells (a battery of two cells)

A battery ready for use in a circuit

Pairs of cells wrongly connected

Fig. 24.1

Unit 24 continued

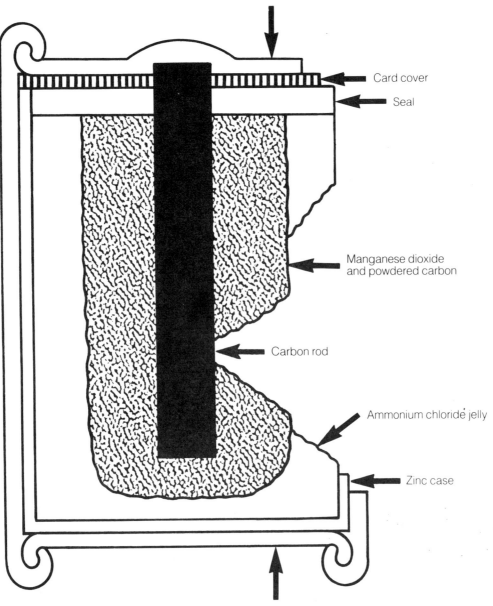

Metal cover (+ terminal)

Card cover

Seal

Manganese dioxide and powdered carbon

Carbon rod

Ammonium chloride jelly

Zinc case

Metal cover (− terminal)

Fig. 24.2 The dry cell

24.4 Types of cell

Primary cells: they change stored chemical energy into electrical energy in a way that cannot be reversed. They are thrown away when the chemicals have been used up. These are commonly available as dry cells for use in torches, etc.

Secondary cells: these also change stored chemical energy into electrical energy. This time the chemicals are specially chosen so that the reaction can be reversed, and the cell used again and again. These cells are known as **storage cells** or **accumulators**.

Solar cells: they convert light energy directly into electricity.

Thermocouple: this converts heat energy directly into electricity.

24.5 The dry cell

The common dry cell (zinc/carbon) started life as a wet cell. It used to be made with ammonium chloride solution. A method was found to change this into a jelly as it proved very inconvenient to have a liquid sloshing around. As a 'dry' cell it is a much more portable source of electricity. Fig. 24.2 shows the internal arrangement of a zinc/carbon cell.

Activities

Do not try any of the following electricity experiments in this book using mains electricity as your supply. Mains electricity is dangerous!

1 This experiment is best done in a workshop or garage. It can be messy!

You will need the following apparatus for this experiment:

    1 dry cell (1.5 V)
    a hacksaw
    the use of a vice

Put the bottom of the cell in the vice and tighten it up. Place the hacksaw blade just to the side of the positive terminal cap on the top. Saw carefully down through the cell. Can you identify the various parts from Fig. 24.2? Are there any changes or slight differences from the diagram? Make a labelled drawing of your cell. Save all the pieces. **When you have cleared away, wash your hands**.

2 In addition to the pieces from Activity 1 you will need:

    two lengths of wire (15 cm)
    some sellotape
    a pair of pliers
    a lemon

From the parts of the dry cell left over from Activity 1 pull off the carbon rod, and with the pliers remove a strip of the zinc casing about 1 cm × 5 cm. Use the pliers again to remove about 1 cm of insulation from both ends of one wire. With the sellotape carefully stick one end of the wire to the carbon rod. Do the same for the zinc strip and the other wire.

Roll the lemon until the inside has become very mushy. Make two small cuts, about 1 cm apart, in the peel of the lemon. Insert the carbon rod deeply into one cut and the zinc strip deeply into the other cut. Make sure they do not touch inside the lemon. You should now have two separate, bare ends of wire available for use (see Fig. 24.3). Touch both of them to your tongue! What have you done? Throw the lemon away when you have finished, but keep the two wires, the zinc strip and the carbon rod.

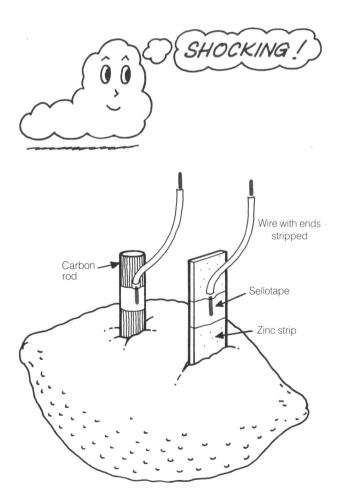

Fig. 24.3 The lemon cell

Activities continued

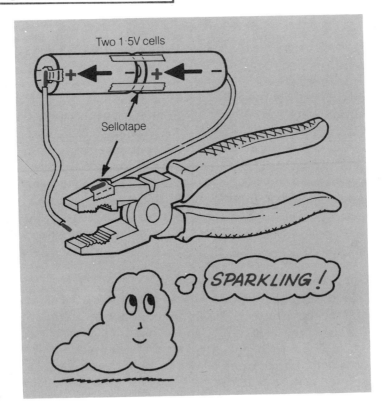

Two 1·5V cells

Sellotape

SPARKLING!

Fig. 24.4 Short-circuits

3 You now need:
   two wires (see Activity 2)
   two cells
   some sellotape
   a pair of pliers

Sellotape the two cells together to make a battery. Sellotape the wires to the two terminal ends. Hold the bare end of one wire tightly against the metal of the pliers (see Fig. 24.4).

Darken the room! Rub the second wire against the teeth of the pliers. You have created a short circuit. What do you see? Can you explain the observations? What will happen if you continue this for a long time?

4 See if you can find some old **batteries** from around the home – **not** car batteries. Open them up as you did the dry cell. (You may not need to cut them.) Is there any connection between the number of cells and the **voltage** value printed on the side? Draw their circuit symbols (to show the number of cells) and label them with their voltage value.

5 Car batteries are examples of accumulators. What can you find out about them?

6 Collect these tools and pieces of equipment for the series of activities in the electricity sections. You may have to buy some of them, but they are not very expensive:
   a length of copper wire (about 3 m)
   a box of drawing pins
   some paper clips
   sellotape
   pliers or wire cutters
   a wooden board (about 30 cm × 30 cm)
   4 × 1.5 V dry cells
   3 × torch bulbs (about 2.5 V)
   one LED (light emitting diode)
   some 10 ohm resistors

Summary

A cell is a source of electricity. Cells connected together form a battery. Short-circuits should be avoided, as they will drain away the electrical energy.

Unit 25

Circuit-board project

25.1 Making the board

The diagrams in this Unit show details of the construction of a circuit board that will let you carry out all the remaining electricity experiments. You can find the list of requirements in Unit 24, Activity 6.

Wires: if the wire is a single strand, then there is no need to twist the ends. Many-stranded wire can become awkward to use if the ends are not twisted (Fig. 25.1). You will probably need 15 pieces of wire to start with. Use the cutters or pliers to cut and trim them.

Bulbs (with connectors): make up three of these (see Fig. 25.1). Check them with one of the cells to see that they are working.

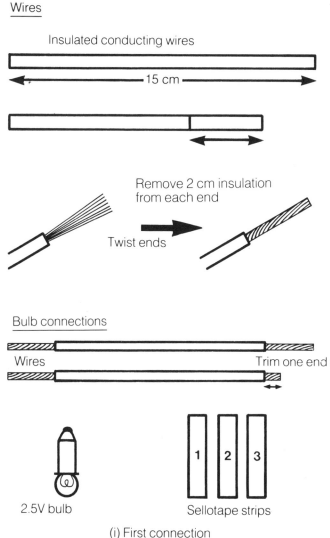

Wires

Insulated conducting wires

15 cm

Remove 2 cm insulation from each end

Twist ends

Bulb connections

Wires   Trim one end only to 0.5 cm

2.5V bulb   Sellotape strips

1 2 3

(i) First connection

Sellotape 1

(ii) Second connection

Sellotape 2

Short-ended wire

(iii) Third connection

Sellotape 3

Bulb

Circuit signal

Fig. 25.1

Unit 25 continued

Cells and batteries: Fig. 25.2 shows an example of a single cell and a battery of two cells held together by sellotape. These will need to be separated and put together in various ways. The later activities and circuit diagrams will show you what is needed.

The board: the suggested layout (Fig. 25.2) shows four rows each with four connectors. It is often useful to have several switches. One has been included at the end of each row; note that a switch is made by joining two connectors with a paper clip (Fig. 25.3). The paper clips allow springy connections that hold wires tightly. It makes them easy to remove too. (Fig. 25.2 shows one of the bulbs inserted into a pair of connectors.)

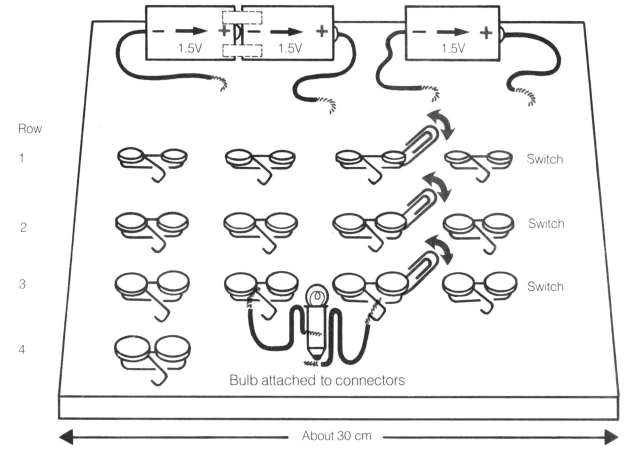

Fig. 25.2 Suggested board layout

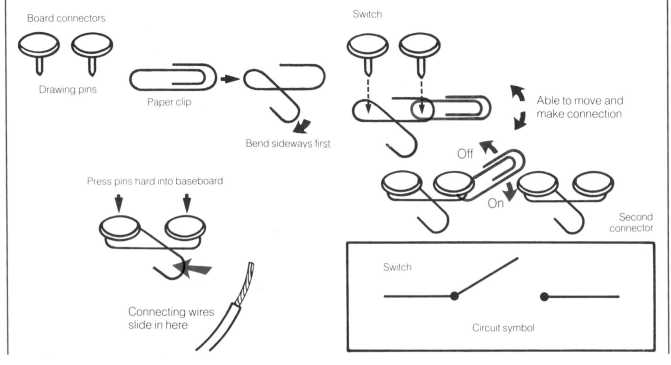

Fig. 25.3 Board connectors and switches

Unit 26

Circuits and switches

26.1 Completing circuits

Light is emitted from a bulb and is gone! Heat is emitted from a fire and is gone! When these two examples of energy have left their source they can be forgotten about. Electricity is different. It travels from place to place by special pathways. If the pathway is broken or incomplete then electricity will not flow. This may seem an obvious statement to make, but it is so easily forgotten. As you will see more fully later on in this book, electricity leaves a source with some energy, is made to do something useful, then **returns** to the source 'exhausted', having used up all its energy. A complete circuit is essential.

26.2 Switches

These simple devices are too easily forgotten. They perform two vital tasks.

(a) They are a safety device. They provide a protection against electric shocks. (The higher the voltage values you use, the more necessary they become.)

(b) They provide a quick and easy way of switching off the flow of electricity. In this way they help to extend the life of the cell or battery.

> **You should build switches into every circuit from now on.**

It is good practice to connect the switch to the positive (live) terminal.

26.3 Truth tables

Many of the circuits that we will deal with contain several bulbs and several switches. Truth tables are very useful as they tell us how switches control part or all of a circuit. Table 26.1 shows the truth table for a very simple circuit.

1 Means the bulb is ON
0 Means the bulb is OFF

Table 26.1

26.4 Conductor or insulator?

Electricity travels through materials in a similar way to heat. Electricity is 'passed on' too, but it is not a vibration this time. Anything that allows electricity to flow is a **conductor**. Anything that does not is an **insulator**. For a list of heat conductors and insulators look back to Unit 17. Conductors of heat are often conductors of electricity too! (Pure water is an insulator, but it can be made to conduct quite easily. Activity 2 will safely show this. For safety reasons you should **never** bring water, especially tap water, and mains electricity together.)

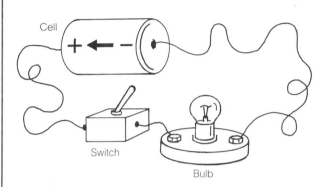

The circuit

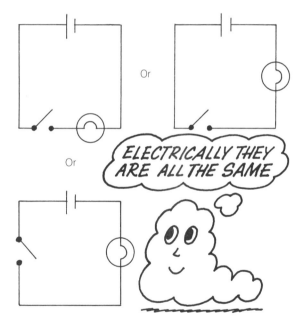

ELECTRICALLY THEY ARE ALL THE SAME

The circuit diagram

Truth table	
Switch	Bulb
Off	0
On	1

Fig. 26.1 See next page

Activities

1 Build the circuit shown in Fig. 26.1 (on the previous page) using the board made in Unit 25. You can check the circuit very easily. From the positive terminal of the cell follow the connections and wires with your finger. This should trace out one complete loop ending up at the negative terminal of the cell. Is the truth table correct? Try this again, but with a battery (two cells or more).

2 Fig. 26.2(a) shows the apparatus needed for this simple experiment. It is to see if electricity will flow in water. Two small strips of aluminium foil have been attached to the ends of the wires and then these have been dipped into some warm water. When you have built the circuit check it by following it around with your finger. It is another single loop.

Fig. 26.2(b) shows a circuit diagram for the circuit. What happens in the water around the foil when the circuit is switched on?

Add a small amount of table salt. Watch again. Is there any difference? Try the experiment again with a carbon rod in place of one of the aluminium strips. Does it make any difference if the battery terminals are reversed? Does this experiment give you any evidence that water will 'conduct' electricity?

Change the circuit to include a bulb (Fig. 26.2(c)). Repeat the experiment. (You may need to change the temperature of the water or add more salt this time.) Does this provide you with any more evidence that water can be made to 'conduct' electricity?

3 Can you build a circuit that will test if a material is a conductor or an insulator? A good start would be to include a bulb, but why? Collect a selection of different objects and by experiment sort them into conductors and insulators. Are all the conductors as good as one another? Can you separate them?

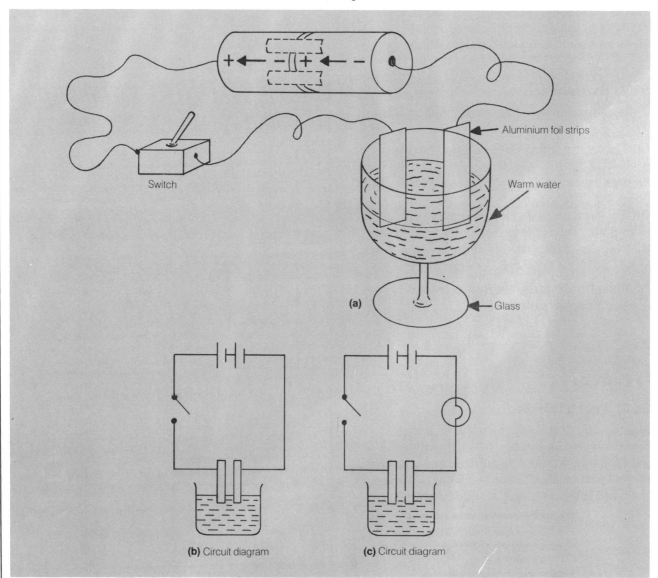

Fig. 26.2

4 Build a simple loop circuit with a cell, a switch and a bulb. With a friend, use the information below to pass messages by Morse code (Table 26.2). Use long flashes for dashes and short flashes for dots.

Alphabets			Numbers
A .-	J .---	S ...	1 .----
B -...	K -.-	T -	2 ..---
C -.-.	L .-..	U ..-	3 ...--
D -..	M --	V ...-	4 ....-
E .	N -.	W .--	5 .....
F ..-.	O ---	X -..-	6 -....
G --.	P .--.	Y -.--	7 --...
H	Q --.-	Z --..	8 ---..
I ..	R .-.		9 ----.
			0 -----

Table 26.2 The Morse code

5 Build the circuits shown in Fig. 26.3, and draw them as circuit diagrams. Copy out the truth tables, and after experimenting you should be able to fill them out with 0s and 1s. The second circuit contains two loops joined in the middle.

Brainbuster

6 What use can you find for the circuits in Activity 5?

Summary

Circuits must always be complete if they are to work. You should always check a circuit first to make sure it is connected properly before you switch it on.

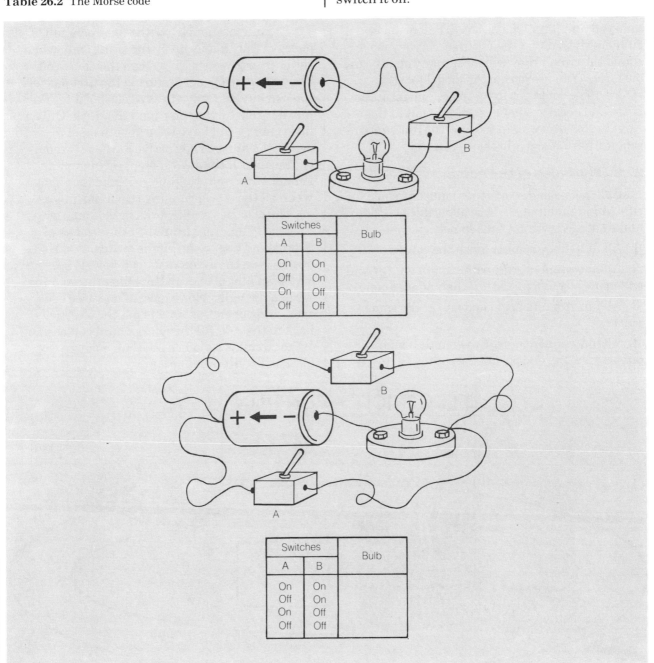

Switches		Bulb
A	B	
On	On	
Off	On	
On	Off	
Off	Off	

Switches		Bulb
A	B	
On	On	
Off	On	
On	Off	
Off	Off	

Fig. 26.3

Unit 27

Getting in the way

27.1 The fun-runners

To help make electricity easier to understand, we are going to use a model. We will let one piece of electricity be a 'fun-runner'. The route the fun-runner takes is the circuit.

A source is full of electricity. A fun-run has many competitors. The idea is to follow the fun-runners right round their course. As they move round the circuit they will meet many objects and obstacles. You are part of the model too: the referee! The referee is in complete control of the route and decides what obstacles to put in the way. In this way we can see how the fun-runners cope with what is put in their path.

27.2 The rules of the game

Like all games and sports there must be some rules and regulations. These allow fair play and make sure everything runs smoothly.

1　All fun-runners must finish the course.

2　All fun-runners start with bags of energy and end up totally exhausted (*all* their energy gone).

3　All fun-runners begin and end at the same place.

4　All fun-runners must travel in the same direction in any one part of the route.

27.3 Ready, steady, go

Fig. 27.1 shows the fun-run course and the same electrical circuit. Table 27.1 compares the course and the circuit.

Fun-run course	Electrical circuit
Rest room	Cell
Starter	Switch
Hurdle jump	Bulb
Track	Connecting wires

Table 27.1

The fun-runners leave the rest room full of energy. They queue up by the start. Only when the starter gives the signal can they move off. They use a little energy during the first part of the run but they have to save most of it for the hurdle jump further on round the track. Only a little energy will have to be kept in reserve for the run to the finish. They arrive at the rest rooms exhausted. (If the starter stops any more fun-runners from entering the race, the race ends when all those still running reach the finish.)

The electric circuit works in the same way. Electricity emerges from the cell with lots of energy and queues up by the switch. When the switch is on then electricity can flow. It uses a small amount of energy travelling through the wire to the bulb, where most of it is used. The remaining energy is used to get the electricity back to the cell. All the energy has been used up. If the circuit is switched off, then no more electricity enters the circuit.

Fig. 27.1 The fun run

Activities

1 The board that you made in Unit 25 contains many items that get in the way of electricity. Some of the items, as they get in the way, use up a lot of the energy the electricity takes around the circuit. Others use only a tiny amount of energy. Make up two lists using these headings:

Large energy users	Small energy users

2 This experiment requires the use of a **light emitting diode** (LED). Connect up the circuit shown in Fig. 27.2. You will probably need a battery of two or three cells. You should start with two (why?).

Try the LED in the circuit. If it does not work, connect it the other way round. What does an LED do? Design a symbol that will fit into an electricity fun-run circuit (Fig. 27.1) and show clearly what it does.

Using the proper electrical symbol, carefully draw out the circuit diagram.

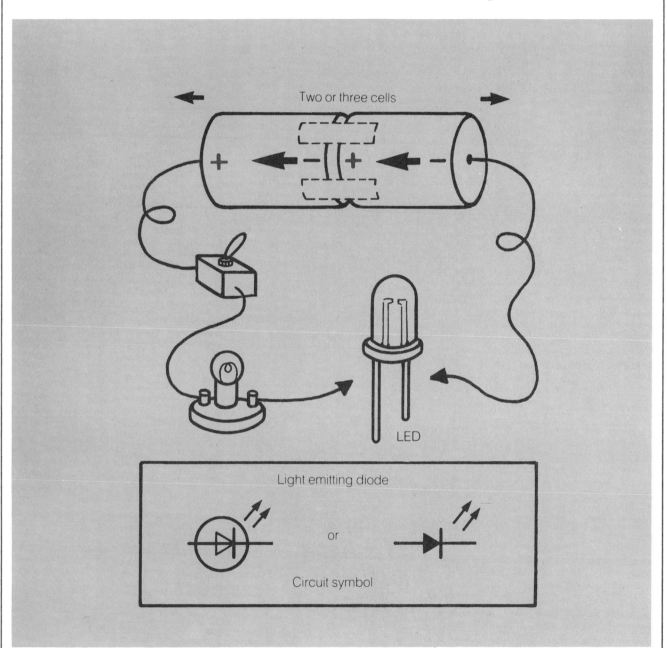

Fig. 27.2

Activities continued

3 The lead in a pencil is made from a mixture of graphite and clay. Very carefully split a lead pencil down the middle. Make up the circuit shown in Fig. 27.3.

One connection from the battery is free to slide along the pencil lead. The other end is sellotaped to it. Place the free connection on the lead as far as possible away from the fixed end. Switch on. Slide the free end along the lead. What do you notice? Can you make any suggestions of how the energy from the battery is shared out between the bulb and the pencil lead?

Brainteaser

4 A modern example of the device you made with the pencil lead is of considerable practical use. How can something like that be of any use? There may well be some around the home. Can you find any?

Summary

As electricity moves around a circuit it loses some of its energy as it goes from place to place. All the electricity that left the source will return to the source.

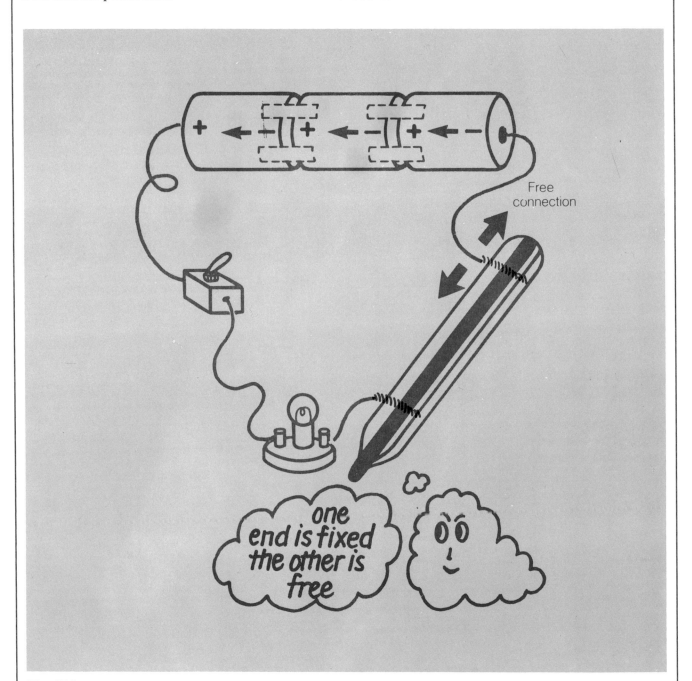

Fig. 27.3

Unit 28

Resistance and series circuits

28.1 Resistance

The hurdle jump that is in the way of the fun-runners (Unit 27) is called a **resistance**. It tries to slow them down or stop them.

Anything that 'gets in the way of' or **resists** a flow of electricity is called a **resistor**. Bulbs, bells, buzzers, almost anything you care to name, are resistors. Any circuit is just a selection of resistors laid out in order. Fig. 28.1 shows a very simple circuit. The resistors have been labelled, along with their energy needs.

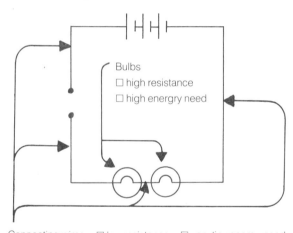

Bulbs
☐ high resistance
☐ high energy need

Connecting wires ☐ low resistance ☐ very tiny energy need

Fig. 28.1 How many resistors?

There are really six resistors laid out. Four of them are connecting wires and the other two are bulbs. Copper is used to conduct electricity because it has such a low resistance. (In this way little energy is wasted.)

We will ignore any resistance in connecting wires from now on, because it is so small.

28.2 Resistance in series

The resistors (the two bulbs) and wires in Fig. 28.1 have been arranged into a **series circuit**. This simply means that the **components**, or parts of a circuit, follow one after another. (In a similar way, television **series** show one episode after another!)

Fig. 28.2 is part of a fun-run series circuit. There are **two** identical obstacles in the path of the runners. Because of this they will have to save **half** their energy for each obstacle. They could not use it all up on the first one otherwise they would be unable to get past the second, and the fun-run would stop. If the obstacles were different, the runners would have to save different amounts of energy for each obstacle.

As you put more obstacles in series, the harder the race becomes. The runners leave the start with a fixed amount of energy and cannot pick up any more on the way round.

28.3 Cells in series

There is no reason why cells cannot be placed in series too. Many of the circuits you have built so far have used cells in series. As electricity leaves one cell it does so with a certain fixed amount of energy. If this electricity goes through a second cell then it will pick up a second amount of energy. (A third cell – a third amount, and so on.) In this way it is possible to boost the amount of energy the electricity has, but when it finally leaves the source the amount has finally been fixed! The energy available to the electricity in a single cell is shown by the label 1.5 V (volts). Two cells in series boosts this to 3.0 V (volts); three cells to 4.5 V (volts), etc.

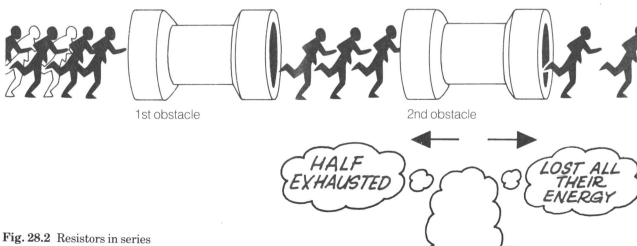

1st obstacle   2nd obstacle

HALF EXHAUSTED   *LOST ALL THEIR ENERGY*

Fig. 28.2 Resistors in series

Activities

1 Draw out the chart shown in Fig. 28.3. You are going to build the circuits and test them. There are many 'boxes' to fill in. (Some of them can only really be done by experiment!) The circuits have been laid out in sets of three. The last set has been left for you to complete. What effect do you have on the circuit by increasing the number of
(a) cells in a circuit?
(b) bulbs in a circuit?
Can you find a link between the 'volts' available to a bulb and the bulb's brightness?

2 If you have some resistors, marked 10 OHM, use one or more of them in a series circuit with a bulb, a battery and switch. By experiment can you find out more about the use of these resistors in a circuit?

Summary

The resistance of a circuit **increases** if more resistors are put in series.

The energy of the electricity in a circuit **increases** if cells are placed in series. The energy value of the electricity is fixed once it has finally left the source.

Series circuit		No. of cells	Total volts	No. of bulbs	Volts used by each bulb	Bulbs ☐ Bright or ☐ Normal or ☐ Dim
	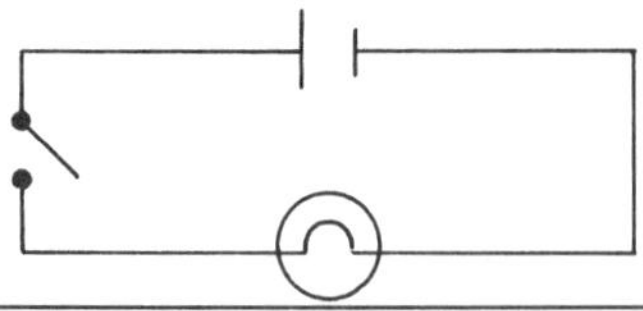 No. 1	1	1.5	1	1.5	
	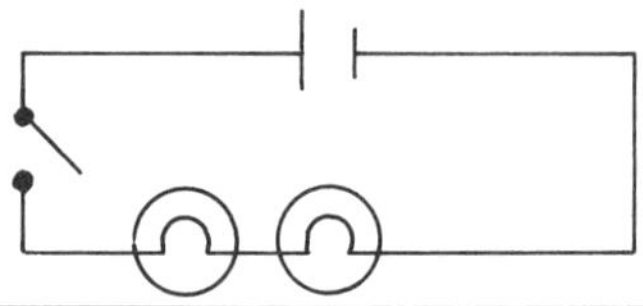 No. 2	1	1.5	2	0.75	
	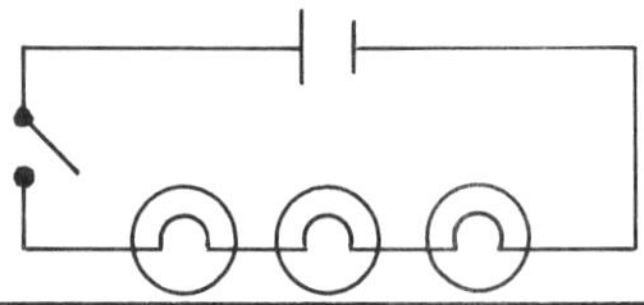 No. 3	1		3		
	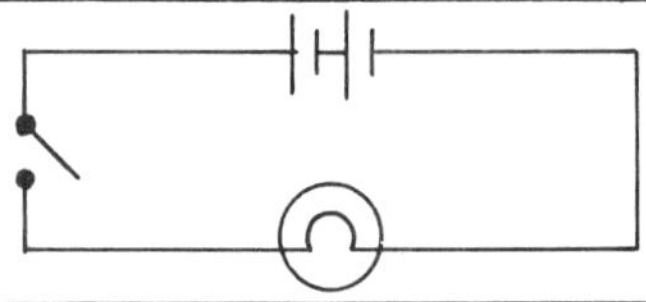 No. 1	2	3.0	1	3	
	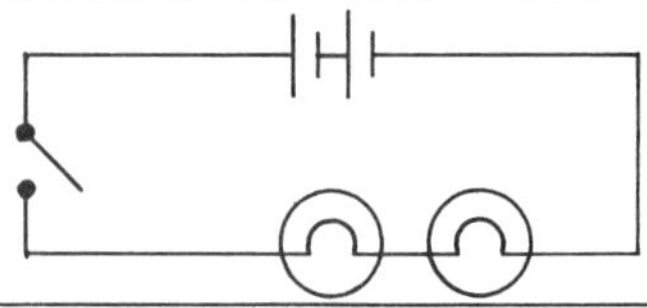 No. 2					
	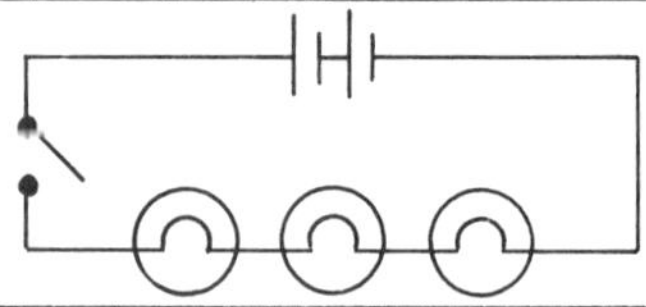 No. 3					
	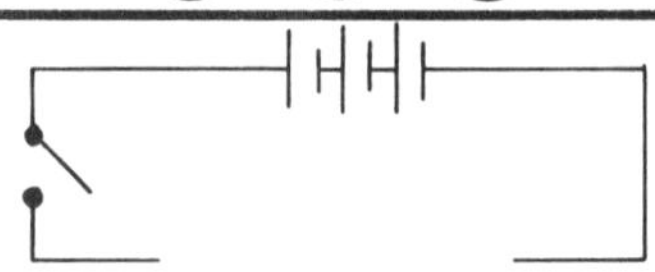 No. 1					

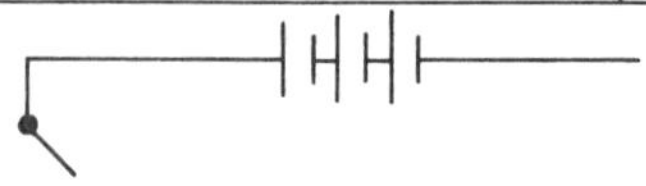

THESE BOXES NEED TO BE COMPLETED AND THEN FILLED IN LIKE THE EXAMPLES

Fig. 28.3

Unit 29

Resistance and parallel circuits

29.1 Resistors

Some **resistors** do nothing more than alter the flow of electricity in a part of a circuit. They don't glow or buzz or do anything else. They are useful because they allow us to control the electricity that flows into parts of the circuit that interest us.

These have a colour code painted or printed on them to show how large or small the resistance is. The resistors you need for the Activities are labelled 10 ohm (*ohm* – this is a unit of resistance). The colour code for 10 is BROWN – BLACK – BLACK (there is sometimes a fourth colour on the end – usually gold or silver, but we do not need to bother with these here). Fig. 29.1 shows the 10 ohm colour code arrangement and the circuit symbol for any resistor.

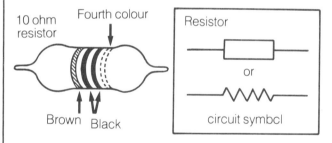

Like bulbs, it does not matter which way round they are connected in a circuit. The larger the resistance, the smaller the flow of electricity.

29.2 Resistance in parallel

If two or more resistances are laid out side by side (like railway lines), they are said to be in **parallel**. Any section of a circuit can be laid out in parallel. Fig. 29.2 shows the fun-runners meeting a pair of identical obstacles (resistors) set out in parallel.

As they move quickly round the track they will meet both obstacles at the same time. The obstacles are identical so half of the runners will split away from the main bunch and go through one of them. The other half of the runners will go through the second obstacle. As all the runners started with the same amount of energy (Unit 27), they enter the obstacles with the **same amount** of energy. They must lose the **same amount** of energy in each obstacle, because when the runners emerge from their obstacles, they will join up again! They emerge with nearly all their energy gone. They only have to return to the finish to complete the race.

If the two obstacles were of different sizes then the fun-runners would not split in half but into two groups of different sizes. More runners would be able to go through the easier obstacle. They would still have to lose the same amount of energy as the runners going through the hard obstacle. They all have to end up nearly exhausted.

29.3 Cells in parallel

Cells can be connected in parallel, too. If three cells are connected in parallel, then electricity will flow from each. When the flow (fun-runners) from one cell joins with the flow (fun-runners) from the other cells the total (or total number of fun-runners) increases. In this case it could be as much as three times as great if the circuit will allow it! The amount of energy taken by each piece of electricity (each fun-runner) doesn't change. Unlike cells in series, the energy value of the electricity is not boosted by putting cells in parallel.

29.4 Flow rate and current

It is important to realize that the flow of electricity around a circuit depends on the resistance in the circuit. A 'flow of electricity' is usually called a **current**.

Fig. 29.2 Parallel obstacles in the fun-run circuit

Activities

1 A copy of Anne's homework sheet is shown in Fig. 29.3. As Anne picked up the sheet in a great rush, the bottom was torn from it and so one of the circuits is missing. Make your own copy and try to include the circuit that was torn off.

Build and test the circuits on your circuit board. By doing so you will be able to fill in all the blank spaces. What do you notice about the brightness of bulbs in parallel? (Very slight changes in brightness often happen if you change circuits around. You are not looking for this.)

Using some of the circuits, again replace one or more of the bulbs with 10 ohm resistors. Does this have an effect on the brightness of the bulb(s)?

2 What else can you find out about the colour coding of resistors?

Brainteaser

3 Anne's brother Edward also tried making up the circuits. He told her that the first four circuits are not really proper parallel circuits at all. Why could he think this, and is he right?

Summary

Resistors in parallel allow more electricity to flow in a circuit than the same resistors in series. A cell or battery will supply as much electricity (flow) as the resistors in the circuit will allow.

Parallel circuit		No. of cells	Total volts	No. of bulbs	Bulbs: ☐ Bright or ☐ Normal or ☐ Dim
	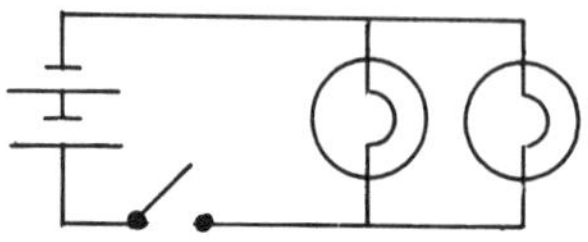 No. 1	2	3.0	2	
	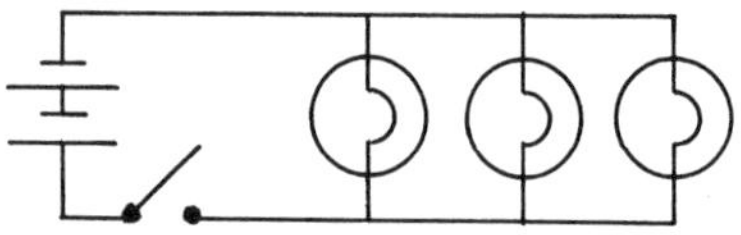 No. 2	2			
	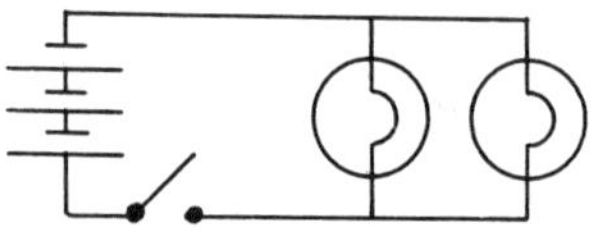 No. 1	3			
	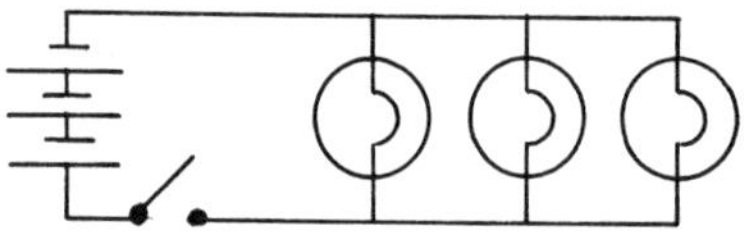 No. 2	3			
	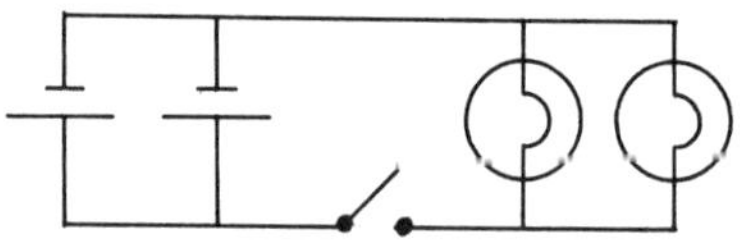 No. 1	2	1.5		
	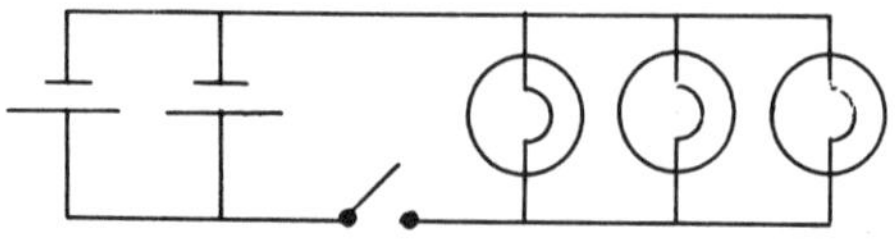 No.2	2	1.5		
	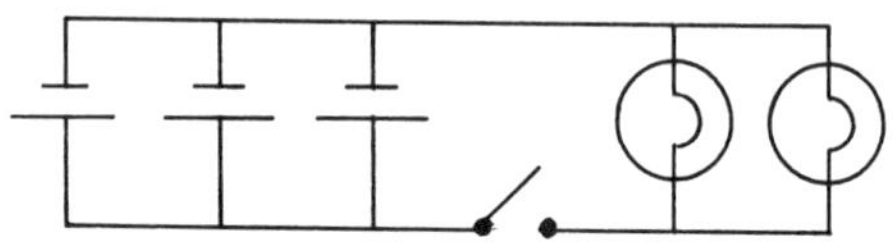 No.1	3	1.5		

Fig. 29.3 Anne's homework

Unit 30

Simple magnets

30.1 Lodestones

One of the stories of history suggests that magnetism was discovered by a Greek shepherd called Magnes. While watching his flock on Mount Ida, he first observed the attraction of 'lodestone rock' on his crook. A more likely beginning to the name(s) magnet(ism) is from Magnesia, an area of Asia where it was once mined.

No one can put a date on the first use of natural magnets. They have been used throughout the ages. Lodestone means 'leading stone'.

30.2 Poles apart

As everyone knows, magnets attract. They also repel. The centres of attraction and repulsion are called the **poles**. The common bar/horseshoe magnet has two: a **north-seeking pole** and a **south-seeking pole**. As you might guess, a

Fig. 30.1 Natural magnetic material – lodestone

Unit 30 continued

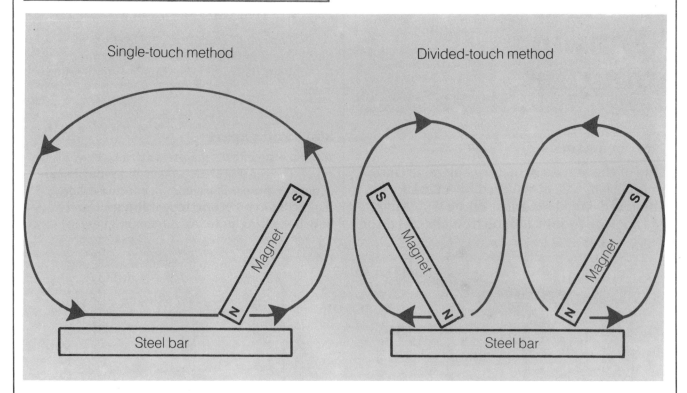

Fig. 30.2 Making magnets by touching

north-seeking pole points north. It is not possible to have a single pole. They always come in pairs. If a bar magnet is broken in two, then this produces two smaller magnets, each with a south-seeking pole and a north-seeking pole.

It is possible to make a bar magnet that seems to have the same type of pole at both ends. This is only possible because the centre of the bar will contain the two missing poles bunched together. The bar really has *four* poles in all. Two pairs!

30.3 Testing for magnetism

Attraction is **not** the test for magnetism. If attraction occurs between two objects, it is possible that one of the objects is a magnet **or** that they both are. The only occasion when repulsion occurs is when two north poles **or** two south poles meet.

30.4 Magnetic materials

Not all materials are magnetic. Some will only remain magnetic for a short time. Others will pass on magnetism, but are not magnetic. There are four common materials that are strongly attracted by a magnet: steel, iron, nickel and cobalt. In addition to these, there is a small selection of magnetic metal alloys (mixtures).

30.5 Care of magnets

The material from which common magnets are made is extremely tough. Because of this it would

seem difficult to damage them. It is, but it is fairly easy to destroy the magnetism contained in the magnet. If a steel magnet is dropped onto the floor, the steel will remain undamaged. Some of the magnetism will have been lost! (Horseshoe magnets tend to last longer than other varieties because their poles are closer together.) Table 30.1 gives some rules for taking care of magnets.

Do	Don't
Keep single magnets in pairs	Drop or hit them
Use keepers* with all magnets	Allow them to get hot
Remember they can upset sensitive electrical equipment	Leave them lying around

*Keepers: these are pieces of steel or iron that connect the poles of two magnets together when the magnets are not in use.

Fig. 30.1 Do's and don'ts for looking after magnets

30.6 Making magnets

There are two simple methods of making magnets simply by touching! They both work by stroking a magnet along the length of a steel rod. The single-touch method uses one rod and one magnet. The divided-touch method needs two magnets and a rod. Fig. 30.2 shows how this is done. Magnetism is not created by this method, but passed on!

Activities

If you do not have a magnet or cannot get hold of one easily then try Activity 7 first.

1 You will need a magnet and some paper clips for this simple experiment. Place one paper clip on the end of one pole of the magnet. Bring a second one close to this paper clip. It should be attracted too. Continue building up a chain of clips until no more will stay attached. How could you use this experiment to compare the strengths of a selection of magnets? Try it! How does this demonstrate the idea of passing on forces?

2 On the opposite page four magnetic materials are mentioned. Cobalt is normally difficult to get hold of. Iron and steel are not. Knives and forks are sometimes made from nickel. How could you show by experiment that the list of magnetic materials is small?

3 Try separating steel screws from a mixture of all sorts.

4 Fig. 30.2 shows how magnets can be made. Try the two experiments shown. How could you prove that the magnet made by divided touch contains more than two poles?

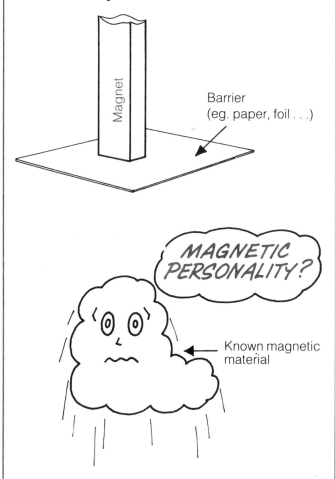

Fig. 30.3

5 Magnets are used around the home. How many can you find?

6 Magnetism can pass invisibly through materials. The effect can still be noticed on the other side of a barrier. Fig. 30.3 shows the arrangement for testing this idea. Collect a selection of materials and find out which will or will not allow magnetism to pass through it.

7 It is possible to make a magnet from the circuit board you made in Unit 25. The only extra equipment needed is a large steel nail or knitting needle. The circuit diagram is shown in Fig. 30.4. The circuit is switched on, but not for too long. It is really a short-circuit and it will drain the battery in a fairly short time. Remove the nail or needle. This should have become magnetized, but how can you show this?

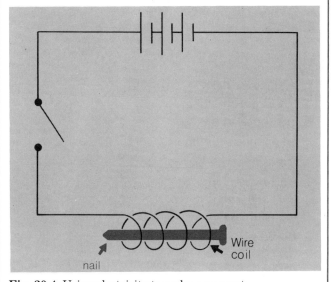

Fig. 30.4 Using electricity to make a magnet

Brainteaser

8 'Before your very eyes I shall make this tiny object float in mid-air with nothing to support it!' said Marvo the Magician (Philip).

Edward, Philip's school chum, had helped him to make the trick. The south pole of a tiny magnet was to be held above the south pole of a very large magnet. Repulsion would keep them apart and the small magnet would seem to float.

Disaster!

'How embarrassing,' said Philip later. 'It should have worked. Both south poles were facing each other.'

They had made a mistake that common sense should have avoided, but what?

Summary

Repulsion is the test for magnetism. Magnetic poles always appear in pairs.

Answers

Unit 1

1 (a) about 1 km
  (b) about 5 km
  (c) about 2 km

2 At 5 km/hour about ½ hour

3 At 5 km/hour, about 07.25

4 08.32

Unit 2

1 (a) 50 kg (b) 6 kg (c) 500 g
  (d) 1 kg (e) 25 g

2 16 ounces = 1 pound
  14 pounds = 1 stone

3 2 lb is nearly 1 kg

5 (a) top pan balance
  (b) steelyard
  (c) beam balance

6 (a) 93 g
  (b) 230 g
  (c) 310 g
  (d) 70 g

8 Measure the mass of the 100 marbles and then divide this mass by 100.

Unit 3

1 (b) 100
  (c) 1500
  (d) 740
  (e) 125
  (f) 120
  (g) 180
  (h) 1800

5 Measure the thickness of the book. Divide the thickness by the number of sheets of paper in the book. (*Remember:* there are 2 pages on each sheet.)

Unit 4

1 (a) 6 cm × 3 cm × 2 cm = 36 cm^3
  (b) 4 cm × 3 cm × 3 cm = 36 cm^3
  (c) 5 cm × 3 cm × 2 cm = 30 cm^3
  (d) 7 cm × 11 cm × 1½ cm = 115½ cm^3

9 They are different sizes of beer barrels.

11 (a) 160 ml
  (b) 210 ml
  (c) 36 ml
  (d) 60 ml

12 (a) Fill the 7 l jug then fill the 3 l jug from it, pour this away. You are left with 4 l in the 7 l jug.
(b) Fill the 7 l jug then fill the 3 l jug from it, pour this away. Fill the 3 l jug again and pour this away. You are left with 1 l in the 7 l jug. Pour this into the 3 l jug and refill the 7 l jug, giving you 8 l

Unit 5

1 (f) Higher, because at the top of the waterfall the water has potential-gravitational energy which it loses as it falls. As the water hits the bottom of the waterfall much of this energy is changed into heat.

2 Kinema – kinetic – moving pictures

M	O	V	E	M	E	N	T	W	E	S	Y
W	K	S	F	H	Y	U	D	K	L	L	R
D	I	G	I	K	W	C	V	A	E	A	C
L	N	T	H	G	I	L	T	K	C	I	I
S	E	F	T	M	P	E	E	W	T	T	T
A	T	O	M	I	C	A	F	Q	R	N	E
C	I	G	S	T	O	R	E	D	I	E	N
J	C	H	E	M	I	C	A	L	C	T	G
K	E	G	A	Y	E	N	F	T	A	O	A
T	R	S	D	N	U	O	S	J	L	P	M

Unit 6

1 (a) 4, 2, 3, 1
  (b) 3, 1, 4, 2
  (c) 1, 3, 2, 4

2

Object	Main energy change
A battery	Chemical to electrical
An electric motor	Electrical to kinetic
Lift	Electrical to potential
Solar cell	Light to electrical
Radio	Electrical to sound
TV	Electrical to light and sound
Torch	Electrical to light
Car	Chemical to kinetic
Fire	Chemical to heat and light
Nuclear power station	Atomic to electrical

3 (a) Electric fire
  (b) Electric drill
  (c) Electric spit
  (d) Electric fan
  (e) Calor gas

4 (a) Electrical to heat, sound and kinetic
(b) Electrical to potential and heat
(c) Potential to heat and kinetic

5 (a) Chemical (electrical) to heat and sound
(b) Potential (spring) to heat and kinetic
(c) Electrical to kinetic and heat
(d) Electrical to kinetic, sound and heat
(e) (Chemical) electrical to light and heat
(f) Chemical to heat and light

Unit 7

6 (a) (i) 300 000 kilojoules
(ii) 350 000 kilojoules
(b) No: some of the heat energy comes into the room.
(c) £2

Unit 8

1 Smaller molecules fill up the spaces between the larger ones.

3 Molecules can form regular patterns.

5 Molecules in a vapour (or a gas) are free to move.

Unit 9

All the questions can be answered by surface tension and capillary action effects caused by molecules.

Unit 10

4 (a) Ship and anchorage; pull at each end; tension; neither moves
(b) Person; pull; gravity; pulls the person to Earth
(c) Screw; push (by turning); overcoming friction; turns the screw into the material
(d) Wheel; push; friction; slows the wheel

Unit 11

3

Force (N)	Object
1 N	An apple
10 N	The Guinness Book of Records
50 N	A 5 litre can of petrol
350 N	You (of average size)

4 (c) 42 years old

Unit 12

4 They are both arch-shaped at the bottom, and pass on forces in various directions.

7 Any air in the pipes will compress, making the brakes less effective.

Unit 13

5 Throw the tool-kit to the right and the action – reaction forces will propel you to the left.

Unit 14

1 (c) Approximate answers only as they will vary slightly with each different graph.

°C	°F
−16	0
−10	12
39	100
60	140
105	220

2

°C	Event
1530	Melting point of iron
19	Room temperature
37	Body temperature
600	Open fire
−196	Liquid nitrogen

3 It is the approximate temperature at which paper bursts into flames: 451 °F = 233 °C = 505K.

Unit 15

3 The thermometers are shaken to return the mercury thread to the reservoir. They would burst in boiling water. They are sterilized by being placed in a dilute solution of disinfectant.

5 *Thermo* – hotness; *stat* – static. A thermostat is a device used to keep temperatures constant.

8 See Unit 14.

9 Continue markings below zero.

Unit 16

1 (a) 42 000 J
(b) 42 000 J
(c) 25 200 J
(d) 25 200 J

2 $1 \times 1300 \times 1000 = 1\,300\,000$ J
$1 \times 66\,000 \quad = \quad \underline{66\,000\ \text{J}}$
Total energy $= 1\,366\,000$ J

4 Water has a high shc value, and so it acts as a heat store. It gives out this heat during the night. The temperature falls more slowly in the cellar than it would do if the water were not there.

5 Jam has a higher shc value than suet pudding so it has more heat to give away. It will remain hotter longer because of this.

Unit 17

1 Measure the time taken for the heat to travel a measured distance to a drop of wax or butter, releasing a lead shot (or similar).

2 They conduct heat from the interior of the engine. This is then taken away by the cold air rushing past.

4 They are made from metal and so conduct heat into the centre of the food to aid the cooking process.

7 See Activity 5 and Section 17.3. The can of orange juice is not part of the apparatus, and should be drunk at the end of the experiment.

Unit 19

2 (**a**) Because the water is warmer it will have expanded a little, and so it will rise up the pipe
(**b**) Convection currents will be set up at the top of the tank. Cold water will be left at the bottom under the heater. As there will be no way of heating this water it will remain where it is – cold.

3 (**a**) Underneath bottom right-hand side
(**b**) Underneath the middle
(**c**) Underneath the bottom right-hand side

5 It is at the bottom because the heated water will rise. Conduction takes place from the element to the water nearby, and then convection currents take over.

Unit 20

5 Warm air rising and cold air sinking are responsible for all of them.

6 It would probably be the time of day when the sea breezes were changing direction.

Unit 21

1 It is painted black to radiate heat away from the fridge.

3 This makes the soil darker, and so absorbs heat better.

6 As radiators tend to be painted lightly and brightly they do not radiate as well as they could. Paint them dull black!!

10 (**a**) Black
(**b**) Black
(**c**) They will move away from the blackened sides with more energy and push against the vane.
(**d**) They will rotate in a clockwise direction.

11 See Sections on energy and heat.

12 8 min 13 s

Unit 22

1 Under a shirt, the holes trap pockets of air. This is the insulator. Without the shirt, the vest cannot trap air, and so is no good as an insulator

2 Carpet is more of an insulator than tiles or stone floors, so they feel colder.

3 Double glazing with an air layer between the panes will allow for some conduction. Glass panes used with a vacuum have to be very strong indeed.

4 The fluffed up feathers are full of insulating air.

6 Ice is an insulator. With the fur on the inside as this will trap air. An Eskimo roll is a method of rolling a capsized canoe upright.

9 Eiderdown comes from the Eider duck.

10 Cardboard boxes act as insulators.

11 (**b**) Oxygen boils at −119 °C
Hydrogen boils at −253 °C
(**e**) *Thermos* comes from the Greek for 'hot'

12 It helps reduce heat loss that would occur as the water sets up convection currents. Heat would therefore be lost to the atmosphere from the water on the surface.

Unit 23

2 Cling-film perhaps?

4 The house approximately in the centre of the row has much more snow on the roof. The roofing insulation is more effective.
Stone-cladding could have an insulating effect on the front of the houses.

7 (**a**) Radiation
(**b**) Radiation
(**c**) Conduction then convection
(**d**) Convection
(**e**) Radiation and convection

8 If the gap is less than 20 mm, conduction is more likely to occur; if the gap is more than 20 mm, convection currents begin to have an effect.

Unit 24

2 You have made a cell, and when you touch it to your tongue you are giving yourself an electric shock!

Unit 26

3 Including a bulb in a circuit will tell you immediately if electricity is flowing. If it lights then the object being tested must be a conductor.

5

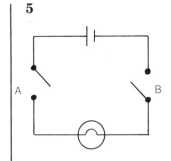 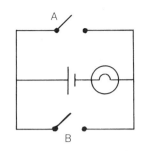

Switch		Bulb
A	B	
On	Off	0
Off	On	0
On	On	1
Off	Off	0

Switch		Bulb
A	B	
On	Off	1
Off	On	1
On	On	1
Off	Off	0

6 The first is a safety circuit because it takes two switches to turn the bulb on but only one switch to turn it off. The second is a typical front/back door buzzer-bell circuit, which will work if either switch is closed.

Unit 27

2 A diode is a 'one-way' device. It only allows electricity to flow through it in one direction. A one-way door, or similar, would be suitable for the fun-run.

4 Control of electrical apparatus, e.g., radio volume control, dimmer light switches in a house.

Unit 28

1 The more voltage (energy) available to a bulb the brighter it will be. Voltage and energy are very closely linked, but they are not the same. So:
(a) if you increase the number of cells, the bulbs glow more brightly
(b) if you increase the number of bulbs, they will glow less brightly

2 When a resistor is included with a bulb in a series circuit, it will use up some of the energy being carried by the electricity. The bulb will become dimmer. If the resistance value is increased, it may become so large and cause the bulb to become so dim that it appears to go out.

Unit 29

1 Missing 'volts' values: 3.0 V, 4.5 V, 4.5 V

3 The first four only have the bulbs in parallel. The cells are in series.

Unit 30

1 The force of attraction must be passed on or the paper clips would not form a chain.

2 Test a large number of other materials and show that they are not magnetic.

5 Cupboard catches, etc

8 The force of repulsion between two south poles is correct. This force is far smaller than the force of attraction from the very large magnet to a tiny piece of metal (the small magnet).

Glossary

Adhesion: the attraction between different kinds of molecules

Anode: the positive **terminal** or connection (electrode)

Capillary action: the ability of molecules to be drawn up into small gaps or cracks

Cathode: the negative **terminal** or connection (electrode)

Cohesion: the attraction between molecules of the same kind

Components: the various parts that go to make up an electric circuit

Conduction and **conductors:** conduction is the ability to pass something on, e.g. heat or electricity. A conductor is a material that will allow conduction to take place

Convection: the passing on of heat energy by the movement of molecules

Current: a flow of electricity

Electrodes: the positive and negative **terminals** or connections

Energy: an object has energy if it is able to do something or make something happen

Energy chain: the changing of one kind of energy into another

Fluid: the name sometimes given to a gas or a liquid

Force: a push, pull or turn

Fractionating: liquids may be separated into **fractions** or parts by heating to different boiling points.

Heat: a form of energy due to the vibration of molecules

Infrared (ray/radiation/wave): one variety of wave or ray that allows heating to take place

Insulator and **insulation:** insulation is the ability to prevent something being passed on, e.g., heat, electricity. An insulator is a material that will prevent 'something' from passing

Latent heat (specific): the heat energy needed to change the state of a material, e.g. solid to liquid

Mass: the amount of matter or 'stuff' in a material

Meniscus: the curved surface found at the top of a liquid in a tube

Molecules: the smallest complete portion or piece of material able to exist on its own. Everything is made up of molecules

North-seeking pole: the name given to the pole or end of a magnet that will point north

Parallel circuits: when electrical **components** are laid side by side, like railway lines, they are in a parallel arrangement

Poles: the parts of a magnet where the magnetism seems to be greatest. They always come in pairs

Radiation/rays: this is energy that can travel from place to place through space, e.g. light. Radiation travels in straight lines

Rays: see *Radiation*

Resistance: this is the slowing down or stopping of the electricity in a circuit by a material

Resistors: the name given to a material or component that has resistance. It resists the flow of electricity, e.g. a bulb

Resultant: the difference between two or more forces

Series circuit: a series circuit has the components following on one after another

South-seeking pole: the name given to the pole or end of a magnet that will point south

Specific heat (capacity): this is the heat energy that has to be added (taken away) if a material is to get warmer (cooler)

State: there are three **states of matter:** solid, liquid and gas

Surface tension: tension is a force. Surface tension is the surface force of a liquid. One effect is that it causes water to form into drops

Temperature: the name *temperature* is given to how hot or cold something is

Terminals: the two ends of a battery or cell are examples of terminals

Waves: see *Radiation*

Wet/wetting: when liquid molecules cling very strongly to a surface and spread out they will have wet the surface

Units used

Celsius: the name of one scale of temperature. On this scale, water freezes at 0 °C and boils at 100 °C.

Centigrade: the common name given to the Celsius scale.

Cubic metre: the unit of space or volume

Fahrenheit: a less common temperature scale. On this scale, water freezes at 32 °F and boils at 212 °F

Joule: the unit of energy

Kelvin: a scale of temperature with the same size divisions as Celsius

Kilogram: the unit of mass

Latent heat (specific): the number of joules needed to change the state of 1 kg of material

Litre: a measure of capacity or **fluid** space

Metre: the unit of length

Newton: the unit of force

Ohm: the unit of **resistance**

Specific heat (capacity): the number of joules of energy needed to heat 1 kg of material 1 °C

Equations used

Volume = Length × Width × Height

Energy = Mass × Latent heat

Energy = Mass × Temp. change × specific heat capacity

$$Time = \frac{Distance}{Speed}$$

Further reading

Science 2000 (Books 1 and 2) (Heinemann Books) — Mee, Boyd, Richie

General Science (Books 1–5) (Schofield & Sims) — C. Windridge

Home Scientist Piper Books — Briant Smith

Fun with Electronics (Usborne Publishing) — J. G. McPherson, C. King

How to make a Rainbow (Hamlyn) — D. Hall, T. Riley